D1075085

AFLAME FOR GOD

AFLAME FOR GOD

Biography of Fredrik Franson

founder of The Evangelical Alliance Mission

by

DAVID B. WOODWARD

MOODY PRESS
CHICAGO

CONTENTS

FOREWORD

FLOWING BLACK HAIR, piercing dark eyes, small of stature, quick of step—this was Fredrik Franson, founder of The Evangelical Alliance Mission. But the most impressive thing about Franson was not his physical appearance. He can best be described as "a man aflame for God."

Franson, a Swedish immigrant, was converted to God at the age of 20. For 36 years he witnessed to individuals and preached to crowds large and small around the world. When God called him home at the age of 56, his converts could be found in Asia, Africa, Europe, South America, and the United States.

While on evangelistic tours, he made appeals for young people to serve on mission fields. His first goal was 100 missionaries for China. Later he sent workers to Japan, India, Africa, Mongolia, and South America. During his visits to Europe he assisted in the founding of five foreign mission societies.

In 1890, he founded The Scandinavian Alliance Mission (now The Evangelical Alliance Mission) and gathered the first party of missionaries to be sent to China.

Carl Boberg, Swedish author and close friend of Franson, said of him: "Christ and souls was his life, his goal, his all-consuming passion . . . Like a flaming arrow, he flew through the world's many lands, kindling the fires of God's kingdom here and there."

Franson was a man preoccupied with eternity. He was so caught in the tide of the eternal that time was significant only as it contributed to eternity. He was quite literally content with such things as he had—and they were seldom more than the bare necessities. His self-denial was the natural outgrowth of his intense devotion to the Saviour.

Aflame for God reveals that devotion and imparts to the reader a desire to be more earnestly committed to the Saviour Franson so deeply loved.

DON W. HILLIS
Associate Director
The Evangelical Alliance Mission

Chapter 1

THE ADVENTURER

THE SOUND OF SINGING met and mingled with the roar of traffic at Salem's doors. A stream of latecomers climbed the steps to the church sanctuary, some of them talking to each other.

"I wonder what Franson will be like."

"Terribly in earnest, I hear."

"You'll like him; just wait and see!"

In the entryway an usher held up his hands apologetically. "Standing room only," he warned. "We have run out of folding chairs."

"That's all right if only we can get in. We want to hear Franson," they replied, pushing forward into the auditorium.

It was near the turn of the century, and Fredrik Franson had returned to Chicago from one of his lengthy evangelistic tours of world mission fields. Salem's pastor, the Rev. C. T. Dyrness, had been one of the first friends to join Franson in organizing his mission, the Scandinavian Alliance (now TEAM).

The rustle of skirts and the creak of chairs died down as Franson strode to the pulpit. He stood beside it, poised and erect, and looked intently from left to right and up into the balcony. Then he smiled.

"When I was thumbing through the pages of my Bible as a young man and suddenly saw the way of salvation in Jesus Christ, I did not guess what lay before me of adventure," he said.

"Yes, incredible adventure, so beyond expectation, so out of the ordinary, that I would not have dreamed what life with Christ held for me.

"What was this life I found? It was the life of a Christian, and you can find it too. Do you say this is too good to be true? I say it is too good to be false.

"I call it adventure because adventure means 'going forth.' Jesus Christ sends us out because that is the very thing He is doing in these days of grace. He is reaching out today to the ends of the earth. We Christians speak about having the mind of Christ. Do you know what is on the mind and heart of Christ? Lost, perishing souls, I assure you! He has a mind for missions. He has a heart for missions. Oh, that we all should be of one mind and one heart with Him!"

Franson stretched out his arms as though to embrace everyone. "My friends," he pled, "don't miss God's will for your life. It is so wonderfully rewarding. Why, a few months ago I was preaching in China. In one of the meetings a Chinese came forward and knelt at the front. I knelt beside him and prayed for his salvation. As I prayed I felt his tears falling on my hands. I looked up, and he did too. He tried to excuse himself. Oh, I felt like saying, 'You dear friend, if you only knew how happy it makes me to see a heathen's tears, you would never think of begging pardon.' I would not have been so happy if pearls and jewels were raining down on me as I was to feel those tears upon my hands."

Fredrik Franson had an evangelistic passion which

could not be contained by one country or by ten. He had a confidence in the gospel and a concern for men which led him to be just as attentive to the needs at home as those abroad. That evening at Salem did not end before he had helped some of his own people come to the Saviour.

This holy boldness did not go unchallenged. The next day Franson and Dyrness met with the rest of the board of the Scandinavian Alliance Mission in Professor Fridolf Risberg's office at the Chicago Theological Seminary. A prominent pastor who had joined their session as a visitor leaned forward in his chair. His voice rose plaintively as he aired some objections to the Mission's policies.

"Do you know what people are saying about you, Mr. Franson?" he asked. "They say that you have these young missionary candidates in your headquarters to serve and wait on you as men and maidservants!"

"This room is all the headquarters we have," Professor Risberg answered gravely.

The minister smoothed his neat broadcloth suit and continued. "Nevertheless, I regard it as highly ill-advised to send such unqualified persons to the mission field as your Fransonians . . . and with no sure means of support. I have it for a fact that some of them are starving."

August Pohl, the treasurer, flushed. "I am sorry to dispute your information, sir," he said, "but we who have watched God's wonderful provision for our missionaries cannot accept such an allegation without evidence. Do you have any proof of what you say?"

The man squirmed uneasily in his seat. He swallowed and pushed his celluloid collar down. "Well, it is just that—I mean to say, how can you expect the Christian public to have confidence in your 'guitar mission'?"

Now Franson spoke. He did not care to defend himself, but he could rise to the defense of his missionaries. "Maybe God can use even the guitar for His glory," he remarked quietly.

After the man had left, the other directors wondered what Franson would say. He stroked his beard lightly as though deep in thought. Then his eyes lifted, not somber but shining with amusement. "My dear brethren," he addressed them, "I never promised you that our course would be easy. Some of these prophets of doom may turn out to be right on some points, and they certainly are ready to laugh us to scorn. We have had criticism heaped on us before, but in the meantime we continue to hear of souls being saved through our missionaries. I think we should pray for this brother who came here today and for ourselves, lest either he or we take offense."

In the season of prayer that followed, the directors prayed for hearts of love and for increased faith. They asked God's protection on the missionaries in Japan, Mongolia, China, India, and Africa.

Then Fredrik Franson cried out, "Thank you, dear God, for Thine encouragement. There is no room for discouragement, for Thou art not discouraged. Oh, if anything good is accomplished through this Mission, Thou shalt have all the glory, and for the imperfections and mistakes we will take the shame and blame!

"Help us and help our missionaries to love precious souls into Thy kingdom. For their sake and for Thy sake we must go on. We are not dependent on outward conditions, for we can fully trust in Thee. However it be, we will go on that Thy Son may reveal His wonderworking power to all for His glory!"

Go on they did, and the work for which they prayed

has multiplied and prospered until today eight hundred and fifty missionaries are serving on twenty fields of The Evangelical Alliance Mission. Franson set the world goal and established the pace. He shared the vision of his generation for the evangelization of the world and did as much as any man to participate in the spread of modern missions. Moreover, he kindled the flame in the hearts of others.

Back in the manse next to Salem Church one heart had been specially touched that day. At breakfast Mrs. Dyrness had listened in silence as the men had talked. Clearing the table, she found opportunity to put in a word.

"Missionary Franson," she said, "today is washday, and it's not too late if you have any clothes to put in the wash. I'll be glad to do them for you."

The traveling evangelist looked at her standing in the kitchen doorway, dishes filling her hands. "Thank the dear Lord!" he exclaimed. "And thanks also to you! I am sure I have some; I'll go and get them."

He crossed over to the guest bedroom. A few minutes later Mrs. Dyrness went to his door for the laundry, and, finding it open, was on the point of calling to him. She heard his voice and then saw him, down on his knees beside the small black satchel in which he carried his few possessions. A pile of clothing already lay on the floor. Now he rummaged around in his bag and pulled out a pair of woolen socks. He held them up and gazed fondly at them. Then, quite unconscious that he had an observer, he began to pray.

"Dear Lord," he said, "several years ago Mrs. Johnson gave me this pair, and they have served me well. I thank Thee, Father. Please send a greeting and a blessing to Sister Johnson."

He picked up another sock and looked it over. "Father," he said, "Mrs. Larsen mended this for me, and she did it so well. Thou hast taken Sister Larsen home, but bless her children. Bring every one of them to know Thee. Don't let one of them be lost."

Mrs. Dyrness tiptoed back to the kitchen. Somehow the household chores took on a new complexion. She sang over the dishes. Later, as she pinned those same socks to the clothesline, she found herself praying over each one. How glad she was that the "prophet's chamber" in her home was occupied by this man of God, for he had taught her a choice lesson.

She had seen that a great man could be unspoiled by public acclaim, that he could still care and care deeply for other simple folk. No wonder God had used him. His public and private life were consistent, and both spoke of total commitment to God.

He had gone a long way from his Nebraska farm. He had called it adventure. What else was it that he had said in church? That she could have adventure too? Suddenly she understood. She picked up the heavy basket of wet clothes with new zest and moved it down the line.

Chapter 2

FROM HOMESTEAD TO HARVEST

THE UNION PACIFIC TRAIN chugged and rattled over the Nebraska prairieland, belching a long, low cloud of black smoke that enveloped the cars behind and trailed on back in the direction of Omaha. It was the fall of 1869, and Union Pacific had just that year completed its part of the line reaching all the way to the West Coast.

Hitched on behind three freight cars, the sole passenger car lurched and swayed like a giddy caboose. Some of the passengers managed to doze fitfully; others, shielding their eyes from cinders, watched the passing landscape. There was plenty of wild life, and they spotted rabbit, squirrel, and deer.

Conspicuous for their foreign clothes and speech, a Swedish immigrant family gazed intently at the gently rolling Platte Valley. Its thickets and woods were shimmering in the sunshine. The land in all its vastness filled their vision. They had sold out their holdings in the old country, and now this was their Promised Land, waiting to be broken and tilled, waiting to spring into new, productive life, the wilderness waiting to blossom under the work of their hands.

A stepfather, a mother, her two sturdy sons, and a young daughter—they were nearly at the end of their long journey. Their bags were down out of the racks and sitting in the aisle. In contrast to the confusion they had met in New York and Chicago, this countryside breathed peace and security. True, on entry to the country they had been greeted by old Scandinavian friends and helped on their way. It was a relief to have kind guides through the Babel of the streets and railroad stations. How close the fellowship had been with these good Christian people from the old country! Now, however, something far better awaited them—a reunion with members of their own family. Yes, two sons and a daughter had gone ahead and had already established a home in Saunders County, sixty miles west of Omaha.

Little Marie Franson wriggled impatiently beside her mother and said, "I want a drink. I'm thirsty."

Her brother Fredrik reached down into the food hamper for the water flask. He looked into it quizzically, then smiled and said, "Just about one more cupful. Watch out you don't spill it!"

His mother mopped her forehead with a handkerchief. The hot gusts of smoke added to the discomfort of her severe black dress with its long sleeves and skirt and tight collar. She sat erect, however, carrying her head proudly, as she thought of how Eric and Frans had been the first of the Fransons to leave Sweden for America, and then Anna. How enthusiastic their letters had been! She glanced across at August, a strong young man of nineteen, and Fredrik, who at seventeen was determined to do anything his brothers could.

God had been good to her in giving her Per Olson to help bring up her orphaned children. A genial, open-faced man, he had been good to her and had also won the children's love and respect.

Together as a family they had considered the move to the United States. From the time they first read some of the appealing land advertisements to this day they had continually sought God's guidance.

One of the questions had been whether to apply for a homestead or buy land. Some immigrants were applying for land under the Homestead Act. If you were twenty-one and declared your intention to become a citizen of the United States, you could get one hundred and sixty acres for the working of it. The very first homestead under the act had been granted in Nebraska. But the railroads could offer choicer land, close to the rail lines. They had received huge land grants from the government in Washington and were busy advertising bargains all the way to Europe. They wanted to draw in people to populate the Middle West. People meant productivity, and farm products meant business for the railroads.

The two older Franson boys had bought their land from the Union Pacific. This gave the younger Fransons an almost proprietory interest in the train they were riding.

Fredrik looked down the aisle. At one end of the car some soldiers, headed for Indian guard duty beyond Cheyenne, amused themselves with loud bets on their own marksmanship, the target being one of the railway's brass spittoons, the ammunition, squirts of tobacco juice.

Laborers going up the rail line as relief crews played cards to while away the time. A traveling salesman buried himself behind the pages of the Omaha *Daily Telegraph*.

Fredrik's mother had other reading material in mind. "Per," she whispered to her husband, "Let's read God's Word for today," and there in the swaying car the family listened as he read, "The earth is the Lord's, and the fulness thereof . . ."

The Franson family came from a strong evangelical, pietistic Free Church background. Fredrik's mother had been active in revival meetings in Sweden. She had started what may well have been one of the first women's missionary societies, and her home was always open for visiting Christian workers.

The Fransons brought their devotional habits and love for the Lord with them. The one thing the children missed on the train was singing the old, familiar hymns.

After a while, Marie exclaimed, "Oh, Mother, I can't wait any longer. When are we going to get there?" She swung her legs back and forth despairingly.

"It won't be much longer, dear," her mother comforted her. Per Olson pulled out his pocket watch and studied it. "Ten more minutes," he said.

Soon the train was braking to a shuddering stop, and they were grasping baggage and hurrying down into the embrace of their own Frans, Eric, and Anna on the station platform.

Per and the four young men soon had the trunks and valises snugly stored on the flat bed of the farm wagon, leaving plenty of room for everyone to find a seat. They helped the womenfolk up. Frans flicked the reins, and they started south along the dusty road.

What a jumble of questions, exclamations, stories, and laughter! They asked each other about the trip and about the farm. In no time they were passing down the main street of Colon and then on down the valley toward Esteina. The oak, hickory, basswood, and sycamore were thick along the Silver and Wahoo Creeks on either side of them, and they could have used some of the shade. Mother (Franson) Olson opened her umbrella and held it over herself and Marie. Her husband and sons peeled off their jackets, laughing and joking, and then breaking into song. The old Swedish melodies took them back in memory to hymn sings by the old hearthside.

At last Eric gave a shout, "There's our place!" He pointed out a roof which was beginning to show above the underbrush ahead. They rounded a bend, and there stood the simple, frame building in a clearing. They were home.

But what was this? Around the house stood people and to one side a cluster of wagons. "It's the neighbors," Frans explained. "They've come to welcome you."

Folks from miles around had come to greet them. Dinner was already spread out under the trees, and it was an appetizing sight.

Later Frans and Eric took the family over toward the fields which were fast ripening for harvest. "We're going to have a good yield this year if all goes well," Frans said.

His mother smiled at him. "We're proud of all of you and what you have done. What a blessing it is to be here with you."

* * *

Long, hard days followed, for the new farm required everybody's help. And until a harvest is in, there is always the possibility of losing it. The day of modern, laborsaving farm equipment had not arrived, and the boys and their stepfather had to bind by hand.

August's and Fredrik's imaginations fired with the hope of buying more land and starting their own crops. When the grain lay safely in the barn and the first snows of winter hid the stubble in the fields, they began to trudge around the neighborhood, looking at undeveloped tracts of land. They found a piece that suited them. "Let's buy it right away," Fredrik pressed, "before someone else takes a liking to it. We don't want land too far away from home."

The two young men went into Colon and purchased the land. No sooner had they acquired it than the grain market started to drop. Prices tumbled drastically to one third of what they had been.

Fredrik was undaunted. Standing with August on their own land, his arms tightly folded together for warmth, he said, "Never mind about the grain prices. We don't owe anyone anything and, if we work hard, we'll manage till the prices go up."

In the spring they began to break up the sod with horses and plow. The two younger brothers worked twelve- and fourteen-hour days. The whole family was busy, early and late, but on Sundays they did only the most necessary chores. Then they rode by wagon to the nearby Esteina schoolhouse for worship services.

Farm prices weren't improving, and some families, with less resources than the Fransons, were near bankruptcy. Fredrik's mother and stepfather were observant, kind people, and they did what they could to help. "Fredrik," his mother would whisper while at the schoolhouse, "go get the basket we brought and put it under Ole's wagon seat. Don't let anyone see you." And he would start off on his errand of mercy.

Chapter 3

FROM SICKNESS TO THE SAVIOUR

IN THE SPRING of 1871, the Fransons cleared more land and put in larger crops. By May, Fredrik came home evenings, dragging with exhaustion. "You're doing too much," his mother said one evening, looking him up and down.

He slapped a mosquito. Then he slowly replied, "I'm not doing anymore than anybody else."

"Yes, but you are a good bit younger," she answered.

The work went on. Then as spring lengthened into summer, and the sun rose in its power, calamity came to Fredrik. He was struck down one day with a raging fever. Fever and chills, chills and fever, and a neighbor guessed it as malaria. A week later the doctor reached him, driving up in his buggy, and confirmed the diagnosis. He prescribed rest and quinine, neither of which were easy medicine for the restless, young man. Now nineteen, he had to stay in bed for weeks, then months, fighting the disease. The quinine was bitter, and sometimes it made his ears ring and his head ache. He grew to hate the tall, dark bottle.

He soon knew every crack and knothole in the walls and ceiling. Lying on his narrow bed, he passed the days with numbing monotony. His brothers and sisters tried

21

to cheer him up, but he could not banter back in his usual, lighthearted way.

They scoured the countryside to borrow books for him to read. Over in Omaha the citizens had just opened a public library, but this was out of reach. They had to tap the scant reading material of their pioneer farming community.

Fredrik had always been the scholar among them. When he had been in high school in the old country he had earned the highest marks in Greek and Latin. August boasted of this to some other farm boys. "We never could figure out how Fredrik finished his lessons so quickly, but he would go off by himself and study. Even back in primary school he began to shine at his studies. I remember one day when his classmates asked him his secret, and he told them with a straight face, 'A fairy meets me in the woods and tells me all the answers.' They almost believed him, and we thought it was a big joke. But when my mother heard about it, she was quite upset. She said it was lying. She even sent a note to the professor at school, asking him to tell Fredrik to keep to the truth."

When Fredrik began to sit up, able to whittle or mend a little harness, August began to talk as though the two of them would soon be back at work together. He could not guess the agony of helplessness churning in his brother's mind. Mornings he watched his brothers tramp out the door, and he could hardly bear it. His mother and sisters had milking, hunting for eggs, and the garden. They could not stay by his side, and so he was alone much of the time. In his loneliness and frustration the hot tears came to his eyes. Why had this happened to him? Why wouldn't God answer his prayers and let him get well? He felt out of touch with God. Doubts began to flood in. He felt forsaken, and God seemed very far away. His thoughts would turn to his own father who had died, whose memory had so flickered and faded in his mind. God seemed like that—distant and hopelessly irretrievable.

Fredrik was an invalid for over a year. He lost his nut-brown tan; his muscles lost their taut firmness. He reached carefully for support when he walked around the house. Inwardly he fought a grim battle to keep his mind alert and growing.

It was a great day when he rejoined the rest at the family table for his meals. When he even went outside to feed the chickens, the brothers were sure he would be in shape to help them by the next harvest.

His mother was not so sure all was well. She sensed the spiritual conflict which was raging below the surface in his life. Her son was sick at heart, and he needed a healing that neither quinine or schoolbooks could give.

He had always been open with her, and she waited for his confidences. "Mother," he said one day, "I don't know what to do. I know all about salvation, but I don't know if I am saved. I've read and read the Bible, but God doesn't seem real to me."

She laid down her knitting and looked at him intently. "God is real," she said.

"But if He is real, why doesn't He make Himself known to me?" Fredrik asked.

"He will," she answered. "If God is great enough to create us—and He is—He is also great enough to reveal Himself to us. Just remember that He is not powerless. Sometimes we get so stirred up inside that we keep ourselves from recognizing Him."

Fredrik cupped his chin in his hands and did not reply.

His mother said no more, but she took every opportunity she could to drop spiritual pointers in his way. These hints were not obtrusive, for she was content to let the Holy Spirit do His work without interference. Her main recourse was prayer, and in her times alone with God, she asked again and again for Fredrik's salvation.

From childhood he had been exposed to energetic and joyous Christian faith. He had heard testimonies of victory in Christ. He could accept no less for himself. A purely intellectual grasp of Christian doctrine was not enough for him. He was looking for that inner deliverance which transforms a person into a wholehearted disciple.

"Let's look at God's Word together," his mother suggested, and they went over the simple truths of salvation. "Can you accept what God has said?" she asked.

"I can't pretend something I don't feel," he answered. "Surely you don't want me to pretend to be a Christian. I wish I could have a faith like yours. If I can't find it, I don't know what I'll do." He turned away and looked out the window.

The cloud did not lift. Even Fredrik's brothers and sisters noticed a certain moodiness about him. When they were singing hymns, the words died on his lips. He would not be a hypocrite and sing what he had no right to say. He would not claim what he did not possess.

He turned more and more to his Bible. Out on the front stoop, stretched out on the grass, or bent over in the family rocker, he worked at his problem. One day he came to the tenth chapter of Romans. " 'Who shall ascend into heaven?' " he repeated to himself, " 'that is, to bring Christ down from above?' "

Here the search of the soul for God was described. This was a picture of himself. The words that followed on the page forced themselves into his mind as though a voice were speaking directly to him. "The word is nigh thee, even in thy mouth, and thy heart: that is, the word of faith."

" 'Even in thy mouth.' " he said to himself, and the import of the words struck him. His mouth dropped open in amazement. Then he repeated slowly, " 'In thy mouth . . . in thy mouth.' "

Suddenly his heart was ablaze with perception that God was not far away. God was at hand waiting for him to turn and believe. The words of faith had been in his mouth all along waiting to be formed. He had been uttering doubts and fears when he could have been confessing his faith!

"Thank you, dear Lord," he said, and then as if practicing, he said this over and over. He was on his feet. He was moving with unaccustomed swiftness toward the kitchen.

"Mother," he called, and she looked up from the peas she was shelling. He smiled at her and said, "Mother, I know I'm saved."

Then to his surprise her face crumpled, and the tears rolled down her cheeks.

"Mother, what's the matter?" he asked.

"Nothing," she said, lifting her hands from the pan to wipe her cheeks. She collected herself, sniffed, and added, smiling through her tears, "Oh, Fredrik, it is just that God has answered my prayer for you."

Franson was a completely changed young man. The weakness and the hesitation were gone. But one would not say that he was his usual cheery self again. He was more than that. He looked at himself and the world around him with new eyes. And he liked what he saw. He was beginning to see what God could do with his life.

         ✻   ✻   ✻

During that summer, revival meetings were held at the Terrel schoolhouse. When the deacons announced a baptismal service following the revival, Franson took this opportunity to confess his faith by baptism.

Quite a company gathered at the deep water hole in Silver Creek. The evangelist waded out until he was up to his waist in water, and there he preached about being buried with Christ and raised with Him too. Franson mused on how much the scene looked like an engraving of the Jordan River he had seen once in a Bible dictionary. John the Baptist had stood like that in the water and exhorted his hearers, "Repent ye, for the kingdom of heaven is at hand."

When his turn came, he moved out into the water beside the evangelist. When asked to give his testimony, Franson said, "I'm sure that the Lord is living in my heart by faith and that He will never leave me. I want to forsake sin, and I want to forsake self. I can't do this, but Jesus Christ can as He lives in me."

Then he heard the preacher speak the age-old words, "I baptize thee in the name of the Father, and the Son, and the Holy Ghost," and he was dipped into the water.

After he regained his feet, he pushed his dripping hair back, and wiped the water off his face. As he turned to the shore, he was thinking to himself, "And now to live for Jesus."

Chapter 4

COUNTING THE COST

SEATED ON THE REAPER, Fredrik drove the team up and down the broad fields, while his stepfather and brothers handled the binding. It was harvesttime, and he was well enough to get out with the rest of the family and work with them as a team. He exulted in the joy of it. They were all in high spirits, and he led them on with his remarks.

Passing Frans, he called out, "Hey, you're dropping a lot of wheat! What Ruth are you expecting to pick it up?"

Frans colored and bent his head as the others shouted with laughter. He was the first of the sons to get engaged. He had recently asked for the hand of a Christian neighbor's daughter, and they enjoyed ribbing him about it.

* * *

That winter as the work slackened, Fredrik took more time with serious Bible study. Reading the Scriptures as he did from cover to cover, he stumbled across difficult passages and prophecies. These puzzled him, but he kept on hunting for the keys that would open up their meaning. He made his explorations like a miner after gold and would sometimes bring his discoveries to the attention of the family.

When he was first asked to teach a Sunday school class,

he protested his inability. His mother urged him to pray about it, and then when he consented to try the new assignment, he found teaching the Bible to children a great pleasure.

The small congregation in the Terrel schoolhouse had regular services, even when no preachers were available. In the absence of ordained men, some of the members took turns giving Bible readings.

One Saturday afternoon Frans came in the house with a grin on his face. He had been down to Colon to purchase supplies. "Fredrik," he called, "where are you?"

Fredrik lifted his eyes from a book.

"Say, I met Mr. Olson down at Maskin's store. He says Gus Swenson has a bad toothache and can't preach tomorrow. He wondered if you would fill in."

Fredrik blanched. "Oh, Frans, I couldn't do that. I've never spoken at a church service."

Frans delivered his surprise. "I told him I was sure you would. I thought it was a good idea for you to get started."

"Started what?"

"Started preaching."

"I'm not a preacher," objected Fredrik, "and besides I don't have time to prepare."

"I thought of that. What about that sermon you gave us at supper two or three days ago?"

"That wasn't a sermon!"

"It sounded like one to me. Come on, Fredrik, you know if you prayed about it, you would have to do it. Who else is there we could get in touch with at this late date?"

The next day at the schoolhouse, Fredrik made some preparations before the service. He placed a glass of water on a small table in case he felt faint. He arranged to stand near an upright, so that, if necessary, he could grab hold of it to keep from falling. When he was called on to speak, however, he forgot his nervousness. These people were his friends, and they were giving him close attention. Of course, it was embarrassing to stand up before some of them. There was his own mother who understood the Bible so much better than he. Nevertheless, he knew he had an interesting passage of Scripture to expound and that the Lord was with him.

But Fredrik did not go out of his way to find further opportunities to speak. Even though he had found preaching came readily to him, he was diffident about this holy calling.

Finally, the Lord moved in a decisive way in his life. An evangelist, the Reverend Nils Haugland, was holding meetings in their district, and Franson was asked to lead the song services. Haugland was impressed with the zeal with which the young man used the singing to build up the spiritual expectancy of the people before he himself spoke. He thought much about this after he left Esteina.

Before long the mail brought Fredrik an invitation to accompany Mr. Haugland on an evangelistic tour of several Nebraska counties. Would he lead the singing and help with the inquirers in aftermeetings?

At first Fredrik didn't know what to think about the offer. He took the letter to his mother. She read it, then laid it in her lap. "I think perhaps you should go," she said.

"How could I do it?" he replied. "I'm needed here on the farm."

"Let's talk it over with the rest of the family," she suggested.

To his surprise, when he brought the matter to a family council, they all urged him to go. They would manage the work. Let him pack his bag and go with their blessing.

So he went, and it was a big step to leave home for the first time. During the weeks that followed, each letter he wrote was a big occasion for the folk at Esteina. They read and reread what he told them about his travels, hospitality in many different places, meetings, souls saved, sessions of prayer, more meetings, and periods of homesickness.

He found it more difficult to explain to them what he was gaining from watching Mr. Haugland in action. He was learning much from this man of God and getting an inside view on the life of an evangelist. How could he share with his family how tiring were the constant travel, the meeting of so many strangers, the responsibility for people in dire, spiritual need?

At the end of the tour he was thankful for the experience and also glad to be going home. Marie had missed him especially, and she flung her arms around him. "Fredrik," she said, "I hope you don't ever, ever go away again."

The others plied him with questions and then listened with deep interest as he told them about the great need for the gospel in many Scandinavian settlements around the state. By no means were all the people moving West spiritually inclined, and even among those who were God-fearing, a great many clung to a form of religion without power.

"I had no idea how great the need was," he told the family. "Some of the communities are much set against revival preaching, and there are places that have no churches at all. Brother Haugland has more calls than he can fill, many of them from small groups of Christians who need help."

Fredrik settled back readily into the routine of work on the farm. His older brothers paid him no special deference. If they kidded him and called him "Pastor Franson," it was only because they thought in terms of his serving more and more as a local preacher.

They did not realize what his experience had done to enlarge his horizons. It had shaken him free of his provincialism. He began to take an interest in the *Chicago-Bladet*, a Swedish-language paper, and other church papers which told of evangelistic activities and movements of the Spirit in the Free Church. He noticed accounts of an American evangelist named D. L. Moody whose unconventional but dynamic preaching was sweeping thousands into the kingdom of God. Moody was at this time conducting campaigns in England, but he had started his ministry in Chicago and was well known there. Young Franson read the stories of Moody's humble beginnings, his lack of much formal education, his conversion at the age of nineteen, and the enthusiasm with which he had plunged into Christian service in the crowded slums of the big city. By comparison Fredrik felt he had accomplished little for the Lord. An urgent stirring in his heart drove him to more and more prayer about his future.

Moody had declared that the world was waiting to see what could be accomplished by a man wholly yielded to God's will, and he had decided to be that man. Fredrik Franson saw no reason why there should be just one man with such a purpose. He wanted to go all the way with God too.

He thought of the hardened sinners and indifferent, backslidden Christians he had a seen on his travels with

Mr. Haugland: despondent alcoholics, vain dandies, flip-
pant young people, and so many hardworking people
with no time for God. They had had a good response from
some of them, but neither of them was completely satis-
fied. Moody seemed to know the way to get next to the
most hardened characters, and Franson wanted that kind
of power with men for God.

From time to time he had further opportunities to
preach. Whenever he could, he witnessed to the unsaved,
and afterward he tried to analyze what they had said to
him and how he had answered. He wanted to improve
his mastery of the Bible in meeting different types of objections and evasions. He rejoiced at every conversion,
but he was doubly concerned when men rejected the
gospel as he gave it. How could he win them? He read
in the Bible that "he that winneth souls is wise," and he
felt that if he applied both his mind and heart to the
business of soul-winning, God would give him this wisdom.

He knew mere wishing or daydreaming would not get
God's work done. Such ambition as he had would not be
realized cheaply. It had a price, and that price was single-
ness of mind. Thus he deliberately set his will to obey
God for the sake of lost souls.

Chapter 5

WITH MOODY IN CHICAGO

In 1876 Moody returned from England to America and held large campaigns in New York and Philadelphia. When he announced that he would come to Chicago for meetings the next fall, Fredrik Franson's heart leaped. The more he thought about it the more he wanted to watch Moody at work. He began to pray that God would clear the way and make it possible for him to attend the Chicago meetings.

The church papers gave good coverage to the preparations for the campaign. Moody was now known internationally, and the ministers of the city were giving him wide support. A new tabernacle erected for the meetings would hold over ten thousand people. The papers broadcast the need for counselors to deal with the expected inquirers. Moody had learned from experience the importance of training a large corps of personal workers for his campaigns. At times he had lacked them, and his only recourse was to handle large groups of seekers by himself. The church papers advertised training courses for volunteer personal workers. When Fredrik read this, he knew for sure what he must do. This was the call he had been waiting for.

"How long will you be gone?" Marie asked plaintively.

"That I can't say," he replied, "for I don't know how long the meetings will last. But please don't worry about me, and promise that you'll pray for me."

"Of course I'll pray for you," she replied.

Both Frans and Eric had homes of their own by this time, and the group that bid him good-bye was small. His mother and stepfather were now gray-headed but healthy. They waved vigorously, even triumphantly, as he drove away to the station with his brother August. The last thing he saw was the flutter of his mother's handkerchief, like a flag held high.

He had written to a hotel for Scandinavians and thus had a place to stay on arrival in Chicago. He figured that he might move later to a boardinghouse. The first place he headed for, once he had checked in, was the Chicago Avenue Church, better known as the Moody Church. An usher realized he was a stranger and asked his name.

"I'm Fredrik Franson from Nebraska," he said, "and I've come to help in the big campaign."

"You've come to the right place," he was told, and from that time on the Moody Church was like home to him. Preparations for the meetings centered there, and the committee immediately gave him work to do. But it was not exactly what he might have expected. They sent him out with a brush, a pail of paste, and posters advertising the coming of D. L. Moody.

He tramped the streets gladly for such a purpose. He could ignore the snickers of passersby, but inwardly he recoiled from the noise and dirt of the city. Chicago had come a long way from what it had been when it was called the "Mud Hole of the Prairies." The great fire of 1871 had swept away many of the ramshackle wooden buildings, and some impressive brick structures had risen in their place. Nevertheless, the poorer sections were still repulsive, and to anyone straight from the country the squalor was almost unbearable.

The Chicago Avenue Church had been destroyed in the fire only to be rebuilt two and a half months later at another location. Now another large new church building had been completed with funds contributed during the campaigns in England and through the sale of the Moody and Sankey hymnbook.

"Moody has never forgotten the mistake he made the night of the fire," one of the deacons told Franson, "and he doesn't let us forget either. He was preaching at Farwell Hall on the text 'What shall I do then with Jesus which is called Christ?' This was part of a series of messages, so he closed by telling the audience, 'Now I want you to take this question home with you and think it over, and next Sunday I want you to come back and tell me what you are going to do with Christ.' The fire completely scattered those people. Some of them may well have perished. He never got that congregation together again. And as a result he presses for immediate decisions like he never did before."

Franson soaked up this information as he did the other helpful impressions he was getting through watching the life of this wide-awake, witnessing church. By this time he was keyed up for the arrival of Moody himself, and he was not disappointed when the short, burly evangelist stepped into his pulpit once more. This man did not preach. He simply talked to the people. As his eyes swept around the auditorium and up to the gallery, each one felt that Moody was looking straight at him. He wasn't lengthy either, but it did not take long for them to grasp his sincerity and the simple logic of his message. What he said and the way he said it seemed to lay hold of a congregation with a massive grip that drew them in love and pointed them to a matchless Saviour.

Franson knew he could work with a man like this. He could learn from him. Like a young Timothy, he listened to and watched Moody as much as possible. Though he was still a newcomer, he swung into the campaign with a will. When the meetings began, he spent hours outside inviting people to attend. He made a point of going after those who seemed reluctant or afraid to listen to Moody. "Don't miss this chance," he said. "D. L. Moody makes the truth so clear and so easy to understand. Do you value your life? Do you value your soul? Then, come. I'll take you in and see that you get a seat."

In the aftermeetings he was active in counseling. Gradually he became acquainted with other keen Christians who were there in the same capacity. They all felt a common bond which bound them together as a team. Moody had opened the way for this fellowship by constantly affirming in their prayer sessions the presence and power of Jesus Christ.

Franson would never forget the day shortly before Christmas when word came that P. P. Bliss, the hymn writer and composer, and his wife had lost their lives on their way to the Chicago meetings. Their train had plunged through a broken bridge into the Ashtabula River. Moody broke the news to the counselors with tears in his eyes. Bliss had been a close, personal friend to him. "Our brother now stands before the Lord in glory," he said, "and sees him face to face. Let us all sing that great hymn of his which we love so much, 'Hallelujah, What a Saviour!'"

The sorrow was swept away as they gave their attention to Jesus Christ. This was the way Moody also used to bring sinners to the foot of the cross, and as the Lord was exalted, they were drawn forward to receive Him.

At the close of the Chicago campaign six thousand converts met with Moody for a farewell service. Nor did Moody forget to have a last session with his fellow workers. "Do you have any questions?" he asked.

A tall young fellow stood up. "Brother Moody," he said, "would you advise a young man to go into the ministry?"

"Never," came the answer from Moody. "If God calls a man, all right, but I have seen too many man-made ministers. I would advise every man to engage in Christian work, but not to give up all other occupations and live by the pulpit. All are called to be disciples and witnesses, but a man needs a special call to be an apostle."

"If the pastor of a church does not favor evangelistic work, what can a layman do, besides praying, to promote spiritual work?" another asked.

"I should do a great deal more than pray," Moody answered. "If you can't work in the church, don't leave it, but go out and hold cottage meetings. If need be, hold meetings on a hilltop. That is what Christ did. Pray God to fill you with the Holy Ghost. Nothing can stop a man who is red-hot and full of the Spirit of God. I believe a man or woman who is filled with the Spirit of God can gain access to the hearts of people and can have conversions anywhere and everywhere."

An older man asked, "What would you do if you were a pastor in a town where there were five churches and only room for one?"

Moody laughed and replied, "Get out mighty quick!"

Here and there hands were raised as the questions came from all sides. A woman rose and said, "What would you do in a neighborhood of about one hundred families and no church, where there are no Christians except one godly family?"

"One godly family can evangelize one hundred families very easily," Moody stated. "Let any man or woman who can read well get a good sermon by some prominent man, and let it be announced that this sermon is to be read on Sunday morning and evening. Then get the people together, and read that sermon; and pray that God may bless it. It may be just as effective as an original sermon. That is being done all through the mining districts. It is a sight in Colorado on Sunday to see the miners come out of the hills and gather in the schoolhouses and under the trees while some old English miner stands up and reads one of C. H. Spurgeon's sermons. They have conversions right along."

Franson was taking all this in. The Holy Spirit seemed to direct the questions along the most helpful and enlightening lines. He liked the rough and ready style of this genial, beaming man. There was no nonsense about him but plenty of ready wit.

"Mr. Moody," a man called out, "would you tell a man whose speaking injures a meeting not to take part?"

"Yes. Mighty quick. I would rather hurt the man's feelings than hurt the whole meeting. Some time ago I said to a man, 'You ought not to have said what you did tonight.'

" 'Sir,' he said, 'you hurt my feelings.'

" 'Well,' I said, 'you hurt mine. I have feelings as well as you, and you hurt the feelings of five hundred people besides.' "

The time passed quickly, and at last Moody raised his hand. "We will have to close now, but I have one last word for you all. As you witness for Christ, aim at the heart. Just keep thundering away at the man's heart, and you will get it, and if you get his heart, you will get his head and his feet and everything—the whole man. The story of the Prodigal Son will melt any man's heart. So will the story of the Good Samaritan. Or take any of the miracles of healing, how Christ saw a man blind or paralyzed and came to him and had compassion on him. Just open the heart of Christ to people and draw the multitude around Him. If you want to get hold of men, aim at the heart; and there is nothing that will warm up the heart like the gospel of Jesus Christ."

He closed with a brief prayer committing each and every one to the Lord and His service. Then he waved his arm and with the words "The Lord bless you good," he walked off the platform.

Long after most of the crowd had drifted out, Franson sat in his pew. He looked up at the big pulpit Bible, and he thought of the words of Scripture which had spoken so clearly to him: "The word is . . . in thy mouth."

He knew the call of God was on him and that he must go. And go he did—to the Mormons of Utah, and to the millions in other lands who needed the message of God's grace. The light of his love for God and compassion for lost men was not to be quenched. The coming years of rugged travel, days and nights of prayer, preaching, counseling, and soul-winning would only serve to make that light cast its rays to ever-increasing lengths.

Chapter 6

"BUSYBODY" FOR JESUS

A FIREBRAND began moving through the Scandinavian churches of the Chicago district, and though some shook their heads at his reported unconventional ways, they could not deny that he was achieving spectacular results.

One great thing was said of Franson. He was deeply in earnest. This was the mark of his praying, his preaching, and his dealing with men. He was up before dawn, and could pray for hours without tiring of fellowship with his Lord or of intercession for others.

His preaching was not confined to the pulpit. Whether it was a home or a boardinghouse, a train or a street corner, he was intent on finding out the spiritual need of everyone possible.

"You are a busybody, sir!" an indignant gentleman cried.

"But you are my business," Franson replied, "and to do any less than to inquire about your soul's condition would mean that I was not doing my job."

How did this young man bring his audience to tears and move defiant sinners to repentance? When asked, he simply replied, "I don't do it. It is the Lord at work. But I don't know of any other way to work with Him than to go after souls."

Some objected to the haste with which he would come down from the platform in aftermeetings and move from row to row, asking people if they had accepted Christ and letting no one escape his direct questioning.

One day when he was reading the Old Testament, he was struck by the words of David to Ahimelech, "The king's business required haste" (I Samuel 21:8). As he thought more about it later, he decided to make this his own motto. He wrote on the flyleaf of his Bible "The King's business requireth haste," and then added a dash and the words "the world for Christ."

Another young man enviously said, "I wish I could lead souls to Christ like you do. You do it so easily."

He repudiated the idea. "Easy?" he said. "I've never found harvesting anything but hard work."

As Christian journals carried the word of Franson's meetings across the country, the young evangelist began to receive invitations from Scandinavian communities to hold missions. Some of the first he accepted were in Minnesota, where whole communities of Swedish-American people lived, whose background he thoroughly understood. He knew these calm and unexcitable folks would be jolted by his methods. Some would call him "unorthodox and dangerous." But he would take this risk in order to get through complacency and unconcern to reach sinners.

His free, unconventional ways did produce criticism, and this in turn increased the crowds that came to hear and see him. Some of the older preachers were scandalized and warned that this young man was irreverent. He might lead new converts into false teaching. Certainly it did not seem to be certain where he came from and under the authority of what church.

At Rush City, Minnesota, a group of Christians secured a seldom-used church for special meetings. Franson preached twice daily, in the afternoons and evenings. People flocked to hear him, and scores were converted.

In one meeting a newly converted farmer named Nelson gave his testimony: "I never thought I would be standing up here to say anything for my Lord. We heard about a colporteur coming here to preach, and my wife was set on going. I wouldn't think of going myself, but after she came back from the meetings, she begged me to go. Everything seemed to hinder. She was hurrying around to get ready for the meeting, when she bumped the stepladder, and down came my pail of whitewash on her best dress. I said to her, 'What kind of preacher can this be that even the evil one seems to be hindering you from going?' She just said, 'You come, and you'll see.' All the way to the meeting she was humming, 'The Great Physician now is near,' and finally I told her to be quiet. But now we both can sing it with all our hearts. I thought I was a Christian, but now I know the Lord Jesus has come into my heart."

Some neighbors of the Nelsons were upset at the thought that church members who had been properly confirmed and were in good standing needed to be saved. They wrote to the pastor who served this church every third Sunday and asked his advice. They told him the evangelist was creating an uproar among the people.

The minister wrote back, from Ishanti, not to let him preach until he could come for a hearing. The next day the people gathered as usual, but a grim-lipped church board told Franson to go. He quietly picked up his Bible and went out into the entryway. There he kneeled down and began to pray for the pastor, the church, and the community. As he prayed, eight of the women in the opposition group spit on him and vilified him.

At that moment the minister drove up in his buggy, jumped down, and strode in the church door.

Franson rose to his feet and began to wipe the spittle away with his handerchief.

Then he gravely offered his hand to the pastor.

Instead of accepting Franson's greeting the minister asked, "What do you teach about baptism?"

"Like Paul, I do not come to baptize but only to preach the Word of God," Franson replied.

This answer infuriated the minister, who then grabbed him by the arm and shook him, saying, "Go! Go!"

"Please, may I have my hat first?" Franson said. When he was given his hat, he went out. More than half of the people followed him to a nearby farmhouse, where they spent the rest of the afternoon in prayer.

Experiences like this taught Franson to be careful about arrangements. He would caution groups inviting him to be sure to get proper permission for the use of halls or auditoriums. He was not interested in needless trouble. When he returned to Chicago, he considered the possibility of some type of church commissioning. Moody Church, of which he was a member, issued him credentials in August, 1878. These commended him to the Lord and to the Lord's people as an evangelist. He was the first missionary to go out from that church.

During the following year he traveled widely as an evangelist, and notices of his meetings in the *Chicago-Bladet* caught the attention of friends in Sweden. They urged him to visit the land of his birth, and he began to give this suggestion serious consideration. He even mentioned it in his reports to the church papers, asking God's people to pray with him about these future plans.

During a brief visit with his loved ones in Nebraska that summer, he attended services with them as usual at the Terrel schoolhouse. At a midweek prayer meeting a stranger to the district named Olson spoke up and said, "My Christian friends, I have just come back from the Mormon country of Utah. I want you to pray for the Swedish people out there. Many of them came from the old country when they saw land advertisements, but they have found it very different from what they were led to believe. It is rough, hard, new land to break up, and the Mormons control the water rights. Then if our people don't accept their heathenish beliefs, they get squeezed right out."

He looked around at the startled faces. "Tell us more," someone said.

"Why, there are thirty thousand Scandinavians there, and they are like scattered sheep. I didn't run across any church out there. They have no Bible teaching. There is no one to help them answer the arguments of the Mormons, and the result is that many of them are taking the easy way out and becoming Mormons. Do you know what that means? The Mormons aren't content until they make their proselytes twofold the children of the devil."

He stopped, and the group went to prayer for this serious situation. Franson's mind was racing. He had heard about the Mormons before. He knew some shocking stories about them, but he had dismissed them as a peculiar, homegrown American sect with whom he had had little contact. Now he saw them as a danger to the very people he knew he could best help. Those people out there in Utah had been tricked and were now defenseless in the face of a satanic system which had ensnared them. Even as he said, "Amen" to someone's prayer for someone to go and minister to these people, he knew he must face this challenge himself.

As he prayed about it in the weeks that followed, he could see many difficulties. He was practically committed to go to Sweden. Some people might charge him with being changeable. What did he know about the teachings of Mormonism? How would he be supported? Could he get anyone to go with him? He decided to write to a fellow worker in Minnesota, the Rev. J. F. Fredrikson, and ask if he would go with him to Utah. Before he had his reply in the affirmative, he was sure God meant the two of them to go.

Chapter 7

MISSION TO THE MORMONS

Thus in the fall of 1879, just ten years after his arrival in the United States, Franson was writing a letter from Salt Lake City to his friends to be published in the *Chicago-Bladet* explaining his change of plans. He asked for their prayers on this new undertaking and described the deplorable conditions some Scandinavians were enduring. "Some who have married Mormons live with a husband and other wives and all their children—often, in the case of the very poor, in one room! To the unfortunate women subjected to such a life—and that a life without God—existence is all but unbearable, and the poor Christian woman who is married to a Mormon lives under constant fear that he might at any time bring home another wife. And what of the poor children!"

The two young men set themselves to become familiar with the tenets of Mormonism. "We hardly know what this religion is," Franson said to his friend, "and we need to discover how and where it departs from God's truth."

They attended a Mormon conference which was open to the public, taking notes and collecting samples of Mormon literature. They noted that the elders preached on morals and even on the second coming of Jesus. At first hearing, it sounded plausible enough; but as they examined Mormon teaching they found that even old, familiar doctrine had a new twist. The Mormons used some of the same words as Christians but with different meanings.

Then they began to meet individual Mormons. One day they were accosted by a senile old man with a long beard who claimed to be the Angel Gabriel. He asked them if they were married, and when they said they were single, he leered at them and said, "You gentlemen better get married right quick, for you know nothing of heaven's bliss. I know because I've been there, and there are plenty of women to go around."

When Franson began to quote Scripture to him, he became indignant. "You stop that talk," he complained. "I'm the Angel Gabriel, see, and you better show respect. Why I'm holy, I am. I don't chew tobacco anymore."

* * *

Fredrickson and Franson walked from settlement to settlement, looking for Scandinavians to whom they could bring the cheer of the gospel. First they went south to Provo and then north to Ogden and Logan. The Mormons had set up a Perpetual Immigration Fund which brought Europeans to America but also obligated them to the Mormon Church. Brigham Young placed them in communities planned in advance, each chosen group having its quota of farmers, herders, tradesmen, and teachers. These people were quite helpless to resist the paternalistic system which enfolded them. From snatches of conversation, in whispers, and with muffled sobs, the two young missionaries heard their stories.

When cold weather made itineration impractical, Franson turned to a project which had developed in his mind. "Brother, I'm going to write a book exposing Mormonism," he told Fredrickson.

They left the territory of Utah for Denver, Colorado, and from there went back to the Middle West. Home with his family, Franson spent some weeks writing furiously. He decided the book should be in Norwegian since this language would be most readily understood by the largest number of Scandinavians, including both Danes and Swedes. "We've got to have something to leave in the homes we visit," he explained to his mother as she brought him a cup of coffee. "Otherwise, the people may forget which passages of Scripture condemn the Mormon teachings."

* * *

Christmas Eve he left his work table to join the family in their festivities. "Uncle Fredrik" had not forgotten to bring his nephews and nieces some surprises from the West. Then he regaled them with stories about the Indians and the gold mines and avalanches of snow in the Rockies.

In the new year he mailed his precious manuscript to Chicago. He was determined to have the finished book back in time for use in the spring. Meanwhile, he did some preaching and organized three churches in the surrounding district.

One day his brother Frans brought a package from the post office. His mother snipped the string, and they hastily opened it. There were some of the new books entitled *Mormonism Unveiled*. Franson breathed a sigh of pleasure and smiled. "Now I'm ready to go," he said.

En route back to Utah he stopped in Denver and waited for Fredrickson. While there he visited a number of pastors and asked them about conditions in Colorado. While it was not as bad as in Utah, nevertheless many of the new settlers in the more remote districts lacked any Christian fellowship. The young evangelist felt moved to write an appeal for missionaries to come to the West and work among these people.

When the two men reached Salt Lake City, they found their new stock of literature waiting for them. Then with copies of the book in their knapsacks they began another visitation campaign. This time they did not go unnoticed. Once the book came to the attention of the Mormon authorities, they were marked men. Mormon papers began to broadcast warnings against them, and it became more difficult for them to secure places for meetings. More than once they were advised, "Don't go out in the country districts. It won't be healthy for you!"

Franson and Fredrickson prayed much about their situation. Was it foolish to endanger themselves? Were they being presumptuous, as some critics told them? Franson thought not. "These are idle threats for the most part," he told Fredrickson. "If they can scare us off, they will, like they have done with some others, but I think they themselves are worried men. With the mines and railroading bringing so many people in here over whom the elders have no control, they are not in the strong position they used to be. And the federal government would like to step in and stop polygamy here."

The two men ranged over the farms on the gently sloping lands of the foothills. Below them lay a belt of land suitable only for growing hay and for pasture, and west of that lay the Great Salt Lake. The immigrants gladly received the books. Franson had written a volume of 212 pages in which he held Mormonism up to the light for all to see. In it he pointed constantly to the glories of the Gospel of Jesus Christ, and contrasted them to the bitter fruit from the teachings of Joseph Smith.

During the summer of 1880 they rejoiced to hear that

Danish and Swedish missionaries were on the way in response to Franson's appeal for Christian workers. "What
we need next is to help the Christians get together for fellowship and protection," Franson said. With that, they
began to work in the community of Mount Pleasant and
organized a church of twenty-nine members. "This will
set the pattern," Franson declared, "and others will
follow."

Now he had a sense of release in his spirit and again
turned his thoughts toward Denver. He wanted an opportunity to speak to the Christian people of that city, telling them about the blessing experienced through the outreach in Utah, and challenging them to reach out in their
own area.

Franson wrote letters to all the pastors he had met in
Denver, inviting them to take part in a revival meeting
there. Then without waiting for answers, he announced
the meeting in the Free Church papers with characteristic
exuberance:

> A general meeting for upbuilding with the Holy Spirit
> presiding and Jesus the joyous theme, the special
> object being to sharpen the vision of the children of
> God to see the bright Morning Star or the coming of
> the Bridegroom to gather in the firstfruits—to be held
> in Denver, Colorado, beginning Friday, September 3,
> and continuing over Sunday. Brethren of the ministry,
> remember the Scandinavians in Colorado, because it
> can be applied here both spiritually and literally what
> is stated in Ezekiel 34:6, about the Lord's sheep that
> they wander through all the mountains and are
> scattered upon all the face of the earth, and no one to
> search or seek for them.

No answers came anyway, and no other preachers attended the meetings. But the Free Church, where the meetings were held, was filled to capacity. As Franson looked around at the empty platform which he had hoped would have had its share of concerned Christian workers, he was momentarily disappointed. When he stepped behind the pulpit for the first time, his friends wondered what he would make of this deliberate ostracism on the part of religious leaders.

He looked out over the assembly. Then his face lit up with a smile. "You folk are a lot friendlier-looking than some Mormon faces I have looked into in Utah," he said.

There was a rustle of pleased surprise.

"Still I'm a little lonely up here with all these empty chairs," he continued. "I can see that the Lord has made up for the lack of preachers by making us all to be preachers and witnesses to His saving grace. I would like some of you to come up here and join me on the platform . . . Brother Carlson . . . Brother Lund . . . Brother Lindvall . . . please come . . . yes, Brother Amundson, too."

After they had come forward, he raised both arms and said, "Now as we think of the grace of the Lord in saving us and bringing us in blessing to this day, let us sing the hymn

Thanks to God for my Redeemer,
Thanks for all Thou dost provide!
Thanks for times now but a memory,
Thanks for Jesus by my side!

Chapter 8

HE BELIEVED IN FIRE—
NOT WILDFIRE

THE MAN IS AUDACIOUS! There is no stopping him." So said a Denver pastor to one of his colleagues, referring to Franson's activities in the city.

"Yes, I understand he has just been encouraging the Free Church in the matter of their licensing a missionary to preach," was the rejoinder.

"Well, I must confess I agree with him there. He showed the church how to do it in a regular way with proper records and so forth," the first minister said.

"One never knows what he will be up to next," his companion replied, shaking his head dubiously from side to side.

What Franson did next was to go home to Nebraska for the end of harvest. He plunged into the work with his brothers with a blaze of energy. Though he was slight in build he was no physical weakling.

Ever since his bout with malaria, he had been an ardent exponent of physical fitness. Almost without fail, he took daily setting-up exercises. This was an era when gymnastics were not often seen outside a school yard or an athletic club, but he was utterly unabashed about doing his ex-

ercises wherever he happened to be. People could laugh
and call him a "windmill," but he persisted in his morning
routine, flailing his arms about and bending his trunk.
The net result was that he was lean and supple.

* * *

In October he started a series of campaigns in central
Nebraska south of the Platte River, a region he had visited
before. It was wheat country among the rolling hills where
the rich soil had just yielded an abundant harvest. He
found equally rich soil in the hearts of men, and a revival
broke out which spread throughout Phelps, Kearney, and
Harlan counties.

Gathering the groups of new believers together, he organized churches for them. Sometimes they came from
varied church backgrounds, but he explained to them the
principles of a free church based on local autonomy with
the New Testament as its guide for faith and practice.
When some argued about the mode of baptism, he said
he believed in baptism by immersion. "However, I think
it is better for an infant to be baptized than not to be dedicated to the Lord at all," he said. "There are many sides
to this question of baptism, but the most important is the
spiritual side. It is all very well for a Baptist to take the
water, but remember that water without the fire of the
Holy Spirit comes pretty cold!"

The doctrine of the church was still on his mind when
he arrived back home in December. He began work on a
manuscript that would deal with the subject, writing
swiftly in a cheap notebook, his Bible open beside him.
When the inspiration ceased to flow, Franson would flex
his fingers and get up. Then bundled up against the winter
cold, he would stride out for a walk along the country
roads.

Again the nieces and nephews descended on the old homestead for Christmas Eve. Franson had received a number of small trinkets and tokens of appreciation from friends along the way. For himself he would not have been burdened with Indian arrowheads or beadwork, a sailing ship model in a bottle, and a gold nugget. He had only accepted these reluctantly with the thought of the joy they would bring these children who were his own kin.

His thoughts were now turning again to Sweden, and he wondered how long it would be before he would have another reunion such as this with his family. He had been heartened to see three permanent Christian workers appointed to the work in Utah, among them a colporteur of the American Bible Society. "Now I have an added reason for going back to the old country," he told his mother, "and that is to combat the Mormons who are pursuing missionary work there. No one seems to know much about them and their teachings, and thus they proselyte unhindered."

He had shared his thoughts with some of his friends in the Phelps Center Church during the meetings there shortly before. The leaders in the church had talked it over among themselves, and after Christmas he received a letter from Mr. Emil Olson, secretary of the church board. "It has occurred to us," he wrote, "that if you go to Sweden, it will become all the more important for you to have formal ordination by a church. We know you have credentials from the Chicago Avenue Church, and I have read them. They will do here in America, but you know how particular the state church is over there. We believe it would be appropriate for you to be ordained to the gospel ministry, and we would rejoice if the ordination could be here in this church which you yourself helped organize."

Franson welcomed the opportunity for this official commissioning with the laying on of hands and prayer. Even though he recognized an ordination "not made with hands" and had been active in the ministry for some years, this service would be no idle gesture. It fitted in with his own study of the Word of God and what he was just then putting into print. He was ordained at a special meeting of the church on Thursday, January 20, 1881. When he was handed his ordination certificate signed by N. A. Stromquist, O. D. Swanberg, and Emil Olson, he said to them gravely, "I will treasure this document, but I will treasure even more the prayers you have offered in my behalf. I believe that your action is recorded not just here but also in the books of heaven."

That very weekend Franson went on to Chicago and spoke on Sunday afternoon at the Moody Church. They took up a special offering to help publish a second edition of his book, *Mormonism Unveiled*. The brethren there concurred in the matter of his ordination. "We would have been glad to do the same for you," they assured him.

"I know that," he replied, "and I considered it. After prayer I felt it would mean a tremendous lot to the Phelps Center people and to myself at the end of my ministry among them. That is why I was ordained there, but I still hold my membership in our Chicago Avenue Church. This is my home base."

During the spring he held many meetings in the Chicago area, the larger ones in the Chicago Avenue Church, but also others in the Scandinavian churches of the city. Pastor E. August Skogsbergh, a well-known evangelist among Swedish-Americans, welcomed Franson to his own church and together they labored for the salvation of souls.

Franson's main theme was the second coming of Christ. He saw this truth as a marvelous challenge to Christian and sinner alike, and he preached about it increasingly. To the Christians he preached on I Thessalonians 4, urging them to be prepared to meet the Lord and to win as many as possible so that they too might be among the throng at His coming. He spoke on "The Seven Churches of Asia" in order to awaken church members to the dangers of sin in the church. He hammered away on "The Gospel Paul Preached" to distinguish between a clear-cut salvation message and generalized religion.

Invitations reached him from out of town and took him to Moline, Galesburg, and Rockford, Illinois. He had a children's meeting in Rockford with eight hundred present. After some preliminary hymns, he said to the children, "I want all of you who want to come to the Lord to stand. Stand up right where you are."

When about three-fourths of them stood up, he said, "Now I want those of you who are still in your seats to get up and go into that side room—you who don't know whether you want to be saved or not. Pastor Johnson here is going to speak to you while I will talk to those who are willing to accept Jesus Christ as their Saviour."

The second group began to rise from their seats and leave the room.

Brother Johnson was taken by surprise. "I can't do anything with them," he said to Franson and sat down.

"Don't tell me you're like some dead preachers," Franson reproved him. "They say, 'Let sinners alone. You can't do anything with them.' The Holy Spirit can do something

with those children. Here, you carry on with those that
are open and willing. I'll go after the others."

And he strode down off the platform and into the other
room.

Christians might disapprove of his methods, but they
did not disapprove of the additional children who that
day let Jesus into their hearts.

In the evening meetings at Rockford, he called on adults
for testimonies of the Lord's grace, warning them to be
brief. If anyone dragged on, he would interrupt with
"Amen, brother. That's good. Now who's next?"

His own sermons were no more than twenty minutes in
length, and then he gave the invitation.

One night when he made the appeal a man in the back
raised his hand. When Franson asked him to come to the
front, he did so but not as a serious inquirer. He expected
to embarrass Franson with questions. When Franson
realized this he merely held up his hand and said, "Let us
pray," and he prayed for the man until he slunk back up
the aisle and out of the church. The invitation continued,
and many came forward. When they had been dealt with
in the aftermeeting, and the evening was over, Franson
remarked to the pastor, "The devil isn't always smart. He
went so fast today that he lost twelve souls!"

He moved on to Ansgarii College in Knoxville, Illinois,
where he was invited to address the students. He found in
the president of this school, Professor J. G. Princell, a
kindred soul, equally interested in prophetic studies. Franson had been hoping to have a prophetic conference in
Chicago, and now he planned with Princell a tentative
program covering sixteen questions.

The professor agreed to attend and to deliver the opening sermon on "Christ As the Alpha and Omega." This con-

ference, the first of its kind for the Scandinavian Free
Church people, met for five days in April at the Chicago
Avenue Church and the Swedish Mission Tabernacle on
the South Side. This time, unlike the Denver conference,
ministers flocked to attend. Franson had learned something about getting cooperation from his brethren. They
in turn had learned to respect his leadership.

As an evangelist he believed in fire, but not in wildfire.
When a woman who was attending the meetings rose
abruptly in the midst of a discussion and began to pray
in semihysterical tones, and then, opening her eyes, began
to shout, he stood up and said in a firm voice, "The spirits
of the prophets are subject to the prophets." He repeated
it, looking her straight in the eye, and she meekly sub-
sided.

When the conference came to an end, Franson bid his
friends farewell and headed for meetings in Pennsylvania,
New York, and New England. Writing back to Professor
Princell after some weeks, he said, "At a number of places
flourishing groups of God's children have come together,
and I found it good to be among them. In most of these
places they are so busy gathering the harvest that they
have no time to enter into party strife; consequently the
sheaves to be bound together have no other binder than
love. I have had the privilege of being present in several
places to gather in the harvest. There may, of course, be
considerable heat from one source or another, but it is
most easily endured when the harvest is being gathered."

Princell read this with pleasure to his wife. "This
brother sometimes talks like a farmer, and he certainly
knows how to work as hard as a farmer," he remarked.
"But I had a feeling after we had him stay here that perhaps we had also entertained an angel unaware."

Chapter 9

ON THE HIGH SEAS WITH MÜLLER

FRANSON WAS AT THIS TIME wrestling with a very real problem. Passing through New York City, he secured travel information and began to plan his trip back to Europe. With a little money he had carefully saved, he hoped to travel a longer route by way of the Mediterranean. He confided this in a letter to his mother. "There unfolds in my imagination the picture of Rome, the ancient world city with its many antiquities and wonderful places and things; of Naples with its volcano, Vesuvius; of the ruins of Herculaneum and Pompeii; of Venice with its gondolas; of the Mount Ceni Tunnel, the beautiful Geneva Lake, and the Alps in Switzerland; and of Germany with its many reminders of the Reformation. I prayed and asked the Lord if He wanted me to go this way to provide the balance of what I would need extra. This He has done through the kindness of some friends here in the East. It isn't a great expenditure. Do you think I am wrong to spend some money on myself this way?"

His mother assured him it must be all right if God had provided for it and that it was the first time she had ever known him to want something personally, apart from books.

Then another letter which had been forwarded to several addresses caught up with him. It was from an American-born missionary among the Mormons in Utah, asking for permission to translate his book into English and print it. "There is nothing in English that answers the questions about Mormonism from the Bible the way your book does. You know how great the need is, not just among Scandinavians but also among many others who have settled here. I don't know how we will finance this, but if you will give us permission to use your book, God will surely provide."

Granting the permission would be easy enough. Something else posed the difficulty. Franson was faced with the shattering possibility that God wanted him to give up his trip to southern Europe and put the extra travel funds toward the publication of this English edition of *Mormonism Unveiled*.

He argued with himself. God could provide some other way. He had already booked passage. And didn't the supply of money prove that God was willing for him to see these historic sights? It did no good. The only decision that gave him peace was to surrender his treasured dream.

After he had mailed the money order for the printing of the book and had changed his reservation to the S. S. "Brittanic" direct to Liverpool and channel ports, he gave a wry smile. "Lord, You know," he said. "You know what You are doing."

Immediately he began to feel better about it, and just before departure he could explain to his mother in a letter that it gave him ten times as much pleasure to get the book printed in English and in circulation than to seek his own pleasure. "If we wish to spend a life full of happiness and joy," he wrote, "let us then do just that which will give us a full measure of such a life. And what is that but a whole life in Jesus, with Jesus, and for Jesus?"

He had found on his first trip across the Atlantic that he could get desperately seasick. Thus he had rather dreaded the ocean part of his journey, only to find the sea unusually calm. The second day aboard was Sunday, and he joined other worshipers at the ship's service in the lounge. He was startled when the speaker was announced as no other than George Müller of the Bristol Orphanages.

Müller came to the front. Though in his seventies, he stood straight and erect. He wore a white swathed collar and a formal black suit. The picture of dignity, his strong, rugged face was framed in white sideburns and a shock of white hair. When he spoke, it was as a father to his beloved children.

"Many years have passed since I first stood in a pulpit," he said, "and when I first did so as a student at the University of Halle in Germany, I did not have anything to say. That is, I did not have anything to say for my Lord and Saviour.

"About nine hundred of us were studying divinity and thus were allowed to preach, although, I believe, not nine of them truly feared the Lord. I had no Bible and had not read it for years. I went to church from custom, but I had never met with a person who told me that he meant, by the help of God, to live according to the Holy Scriptures.

"A fellow student invited me to a meeting in the home of a tradesman named Wagner. I was rather embarrassed to go, but I did. I was not acquainted with the manner of believers and the joy they have in seeing poor sinners even in any measure caring about the things of God. I made an apology for my coming. The kind answer of this dear brother Wagner I shall never forget. He said, 'Come as often as you please; home and heart are open to you.'

"In the meeting he led in prayer, and while he prayed my feeling was something like this: 'I could not pray as well though I am much more learned than this illiterate man.' On my return to my room I said to my friend, 'All we have seen on our journey to Switzerland and all our former pleasures are as nothing in comparison with this evening.'"

As Müller continued his testimony, the audience listened raptly. Some of them had come expecting to hear an appeal for funds for the orphans, but here was a man who spoke only to the glory of his Lord and Saviour. He told how he had been saved and then how he had begun to get acquainted with the Bible.

"At first I fell into the snare of reading religious books in preference to the Scriptures. Now the scriptural way of reasoning would have been that God Himself has condescended to become an author, and I am ignorant about that precious Book which His Holy Spirit has caused to be written through the instrumentality of His servants. It contains what I ought to know, and the knowledge in it will lead me to true happiness. Therefore, I ought to read again and again this most precious Book, the Book of books, most earnestly, most prayerfully, and with much meditation, and in this practice I ought to continue all the days of my life."

Franson drank this in, and it was like nectar to his soul. All the while he was thinking to himself, *If I had gone the other way, then I would have missed this!*

The ten-day trip together with George Müller was indeed one of the richest gifts God could have given Franson.

"A missionary-evangelist!" exclaimed the grand old man when he introduced himself. "Why, I wanted to be a missionary. I applied to the London Mission to the Jews and then went over to England to prepare. My English was broken, but I already had Latin, Greek, and French besides my native German. I studied Hebrew, even committing portions of the Hebrew Old Testament to memory. Those were good days! I looked up to the Lord even while I was turning over the leaves of my Hebrew dictionary, asking His help that I might quickly find the words."

He stopped and seemed to be turning this memory over in his mind.

Franson asked, "Did He help you?"

Müller blinked and smiled, "Why, yes, I believe He did. I moved along with surprising speed. I also commenced Chaldee as well as German-Jewish in Rabbinic characters."

Franson had another question, "After all that work, were you disappointed when God called you to another type of ministry?"

Müller said, "No, I had already begun to learn something about trusting the Lord's wisdom above my own. I left it in His hands, and that preparation was never wasted."

Franson felt a kinship with this man who had also come to Christ through great struggle and lived most of his days in an adopted country. Most of all, he admired the rigorous faith and daring of this aged saint. Müller was not resting on his laurels; he was still facing new tests of faith.

"My dear friend," he said, as he continued to reminisce, "I constantly had cases brought before me which proved that one of the special things which the children of God need in our day is to have their faith strengthened. I

longed to have something to point to as a visible proof that
our God and Father is the same faithful God as He ever
was, as willing as ever to prove Himself to be the living
God, in our day as formerly, to all who put their trust in
Him. I longed to set something before the children of
God whereby they might see that He does not forsake,
even in our day, those who rely upon Him. I had obtained
so much mercy at His hands in being able to take Him at
His word and to rely upon it that I felt bound to serve the
church of God at this particular point. And the more I
have lived this life the more I have seen the need of it.
Not that every Christian should be without salary and
make his needs known to God alone, but that each one of
us should have confidence in God for every area of our
lives."

Franson shared with Müller his own experiences in
trusting the Lord to supply his needs as an evangelist in
America. When he told him his evangelistic objectives in
the months ahead, Müller carefully jotted the details
down. "I will be praying for you, my brother," he
promised, "and do remember this one last word of advice:
In your church order, in your public life, in your private
life, just have one rule, and that is What does the
Bible say?"

History has no way of recording the effectiveness of
Müller's prayers for the young missionary-evangelist, but
it is probable that they contributed greatly to Franson's
worldwide soul-winning ministry.

Chapter 10

SWEDEN FOR CHRIST

At Liverpool Franson bade Müller good-bye. "I shall never forget what you have told me about what has been accomplished through faith and prayer," he said.

"Faith and prayer only, faith and prayer only," intoned the old man.

Franson himself had an immediate decision to pray about. He found he could get passage directly to Sweden or continue to Hamburg and travel up through Denmark toward his old homeland. He chose the latter because it would enable him to visit Copenhagen. There the Mormons had their headquarters and publishing house for Scandinavia.

He had a plan in mind. If he could learn the location of Mormon missionary work in various cities, he would mail copies of his book to churches and mission societies in those places to help them combat the propaganda of this false sect.

One sunny day in June he walked into the main office of the "Church of Latter-Day Saints." He approached the reception desk and asked the young man there, "Would you please give me information about your centers or work in Scandinavia? I would like to know where you have meeting places."

The Mormon missionary smiled pleasantly and began to reach into a drawer of his desk for a magazine which listed this information. He was interrupted by another man who came bounding up from behind. "Stop!" he said. "I know this man."

Addressing Franson, he angrily asked, "What do you want in here?"

His voice brought other members of the office staff from their desks. Franson looked around him calmly. "I only came in to ask for some information which is no great secret," he said.

"You're up to no good," his opponent replied, "I know you. I heard you speak in Utah where you went around warning people against our religion. What are you doing here?"

Franson looked straight at him. "I have come to Scandinavia to do the same work I have been engaged in for some years, and that is preaching the gospel of Jesus Christ."

This announcement infuriated the other man. "Listen here, what's your name?" he asked. "If you try to influence people and attack what we've been doing, we'll find means of silencing you."

A murmur of approval greeted this threat, and the group of office workers moved in closer.

The man raised his arm as though to strike Franson. "Promise me that you won't attack our church doctrines," he ordered.

"I'll give you no such guarantee," Franson answered.

"You—you—" the man sputtered, but words failed him.

The others pressed forward. "Get out! Get out!" they cried and pushed him out the door and into the street.

The report of this encounter preceded Franson to

Malmo, and when he reached this Swedish port, he was greeted with keen interest. "We hear that wherever you go there is either a riot or a revival," one Christian brother said, "and already over in Copenhagen it has begun."

"I do not aim at provoking riots," Franson replied, "but I do pray for revival. You have had the news of how the Mormons opposed me. Listen now as I tell you how God worked in hearts during the few days I was in Denmark."

His words fell like sparks on tinder, and that very night revival began in his native Sweden. It was Pentecost Sunday, and the meetings commenced that day continued for two weeks in various churches of the city. He went on to Stockholm, the capital, for the annual conference of the Swedish Mission Covenant Church, there to meet many faithful Christian workers from all over the country. Many of them invited him to come and preach in their churches. "First I must go to my old home in Nora," he said, "for I have relatives and friends there."

He had left at 17 and was returning at the age of 29. He was remembered as a shy schoolboy, and now he was instead a rather notorious figure. He was awaited with much suspicion and curiosity. Even his relatives eyed him critically. Would he disgrace them in public and make them wish he had never come back?

Franson plunged into meetings, and people crowded to hear him. He was dignified on the platform, but obviously he was buoyed up with a special joy at being with old friends and classmates. He began to win their hearts, and his supporters were earnest in his defense. "You know that he is sincere," they said. "We should overlook his unusual way of conducting aftermeetings. His heart is full and he speaks of his convictions only to share his own happiness with others."

Some argued differently, saying, "He should have more consideration for our way of worship and not give offense. After all, we have been accustomed to reverence in worship all our lives."

"Yes, but even if you don't agree with him, you should respect him," was the answer. "If a political speaker comes along, you honor him for his principles even if you don't accept them, and you should honor a religious speaker in the same way."

One day Franson's old principal, Ernest Brandberg, attended one of his meetings. Fredrik had been a favorite pupil of his, and he had marked him for success. He did not approve of evangelism, however, and was disappointed that this former student should have turned into a revival preacher. His ears were not open to hear the message. He could see nothing to commend in Franson's performance. As Brandberg left the hall without a word of greeting to Franson, some of his students followed him to hear his opinion. He rested both hands on his cane and surveyed them. "Theatrical!" he pontificated. "I never thought I would live to see such bad taste."

That very night his remarks reached Franson, and they wounded him as they were intended to do. "It hurts," he said to his friends, "I won't pretend that it doesn't hurt. I would have liked to enjoy now the same relationship we once had. I suppose it hurts him that I no longer look to him as my chief teacher. Ever since the Holy Spirit became my Teacher, I have had to change a lot of my own way of thinking.

"Nevertheless, I keep asking the Lord if I am doing things in the wrong way when I hear these complaints. Already I have heard many times in this country the objection that my methods are foreign and don't fit the national character of Swedes. It is true that everything that is spiritual will not agree with you people or with the human nature in any country. But I notice that when people become partakers of God's nature and character, the aftermeetings agree with them very well. Whatever the Bible teaches is going to be suitable for every nation. The Bible teaches men to repent and be saved. If anybody is going to call this a way or a method, all I can say is that it is better to be saved the American way than to be lost the European way!"

"Brother Franson, we agree with you," a friend stated, "but we can see problems ahead. As long as we free church people worship quietly and go about our business, the laws of the State against us are not applied. When someone comes along and creates such a stir as you do in your meetings, it brings you to public notice."

"What effect do you think that will have?" he asked.

"The powers that be don't like it, and they will try to stop you. After all, 99 out of 100 citizens are nominal members of the state church. Being baptized and confirmed is just standard practice for any good, law-abiding, patriotic citizen. You are outside the established church, and your ordination will not be recognized. In a sense, you are an outcast."

"Glory be! That sounds more and more like the Lord and His disciples."

And with that Franson set his face toward a confrontation with the opposition, for he was not willing to stop seeking souls. He would not, for the sake of peace, quit using the Sword of the Spirit.

Hundreds turned to Christ during the next weeks, many of them in meetings, but others through brief encounters with Franson.

One day he stopped at the town of Boras to see a grocer about meeting arrangements for the following week. Then leaving hastily, he headed toward the door. A lady came toward him at that moment, so he held the door open for her. She thanked him for his courtesy. "Madame," he replied, "are you saved?"

"Saved?"

"Yes, do you know Jesus Christ?"

"Why, He's the Son of God."

"Do you love Him?"

"I'm afraid not."

"Don't you think you ought to?"

"Yes."

"Well, if you do, be rapid about it because my train leaves in five minutes." And down they went on their knees, and he led that lady to the Lord in about two minutes.

Rising, Franson said, "God bless you. Good-bye." And he was off at a run for the station platform.

Chapter 11

CONFLICTS AND CONQUESTS

L<small>ETTERS</small> <small>DESCRIBING</small> Franson's campaigns crossed the Atlantic, and friends in America redoubled their prayers for him. One Swedish Christian reported, "The Lord has truly identified Himself with Mr. Franson's meetings. Many hundreds have been saved. The children of God have also been stirred up as they have seen the importance of witnessing to others. In Norrkoping so many people came, they had to be divided up, with the men attending one meeting and the women the next, and still many were turned away. One evening the State Church preacher attended. He sat still until Mr. Franson began the aftermeeting. Then he told the people to go home because this was not the right way to conduct meetings. His supporters shouted their approval, but to the surprise of the preacher a great many more disagreed. He left with a few people, but the rest remained. Afterward, they noticed that some policemen had gathered outside."

Franson's main theme in preaching was the second coming of Christ, a doctrine which was new and fascinating for most. Schoolhouses and mission houses were always full of people to hear him on this subject.

"In our days many think it impossible to understand the prophetic Word," he would explain, "but Peter says in II Peter 1:19 that prophecy is a light that shines more and more till the day dawns. The devil has tried to make us believe the Bible is a book nobody can understand. When it says Satan is going to be bound, he is not anxious that we should read that. People don't want to serve a master who is soon to be bound. If he were bound for only a few days every one of you would be saved. And now, dear friends, come to the Saviour who stands here with open arms to receive you."

To the newly converted he would say, "You have now received a gift which has been waiting for a long time, namely, Jesus. Try now to keep this as an unshakable truth, that you are a child of God and joint-heir with Christ, as you rest and trust in Him. Never let the devil argue with you. Go instead and find older Christians to help you. Always keep in mind that Jesus is near. Claim the privileges of the bride. Do not forget that Jesus has need of your keeping close to Him. Be always busy for Jesus, because it will keep you from many an occasion to commit sin. I say this as a brother who will bring you before the throne of grace in prayer each morning and who wants to meet you in the sky."

The newspapers tried to understand and interpret what was going on, and their reports ranged from tart suggestions that Franson's head ought to be examined by a doctor to attempts at sympathetic appraisal. One paper said, "This preacher behaves in a way that is strange to us; still one must remember that he has lived for quite some time in free America, where habits and customs greatly differ. Besides, every honest person should take into consideration the preacher's enthusiasm, which, in his own fearless way, causes his appearance to be so entirely different from that of other preachers. But is there anything blamable in that? We have every reason to believe that he is guided by the pure motive of reaching slaves of vice to bring them to Christ. He is also urging the formal Christian to live what he professes. We agree that sometimes his conduct seems far from sensible, yes, even unwise, but we should overlook this and excuse it. Empty forms and phrases are far more dangerous to the church than this religious movement."

In some places where the free church meeting houses were closed to Franson, he found warmhearted State Church men who opened their doors to him. At Linkoping he held meetings in the Lutheran Mission House, but crowds of teenagers caused a lot of disturbance outside. Finally, Dean Linder, the local church leader, put in an appearance at a meeting to see what was going on. In the aftermeeting Franson went among the audience asking everyone whether or not he was saved. Many answered jokingly or ridiculed him. When Franson came to Dean Linder, he looked at the elderly man kindly, as he sat there in clerical garb. Giving him a friendly pat on the shoulder, he asked him the same question, "Are you saved?"

The dean shrank away as if he had been bitten and began to make sarcastic remarks about his preaching and the way he conducted his meetings. Franson looked steadily at him and then said, "I am not ashamed of the gospel of Christ: for it is the power of God unto salvation to every one that believeth; to the Jew first, and also to the Greek. For therein is the righteousness of God revealed from faith to faith: as it is written, The just shall live by faith. For the wrath of God is revealed from heaven against all ungodliness and unrighteousness of men, who hold the truth in unrighteousness."

Then he knelt down and took both the dean's hands in his while he prayed for him. "Lord Jesus, save this man. Help him to believe. If he does not allow Thee to save him, please take him away, so that he no longer resists Thy kingdom in this town."

A hush prevailed over the assembly as the dean got to his feet and walked out. Within twenty-four hours he had his vengeance. He got the church council to forbid Franson to hold any more meetings there. This brought a protest from the local paper. The editor leaped to Franson's defense, saying, "Why has the church council issued orders against this stranger? True, the council has the power to forbid laymen to conduct religious meetings and even see them fined by the state if they do not obey. But such rules are a disgrace to the district and the whole country. Rules made by a church council cannot change people's religious convictions. They cannot hold back religious zeal. Such rules will instead have the opposite result. Wouldn't it be better if those who disturbed the meetings were called to account?"

In the months which followed, Franson went on to other parts of the country, but Dean Linder had not forgotten him. He had started to fail in health and was soon at the point of death. He had brooded much over Franson's prayer for him, and finally he had capitulated to his Lord and Saviour. On his deathbed he beckoned to a member of his household. "I know the people are saying that I am dying because I provoked God," he rasped. "But tell them that now I am longing to be with Jesus."

Franson often took time out from his busy schedule to spend time apart with the Lord. Once, meeting a friend at a railway station after he had been on a retreat, he said, "Do you know, the Lord met me today and gave me new power and promised to be with me in all my meetings, so that souls shall be saved and God's name be glorified. When you are worn out, do as I have done; seek out a quiet spot in the woods, and you will receive a blessing from the Lord such as you never dreamed of. God bless you!"

To him the spiritual battle for souls was much more pressing than the repeated conflicts with the State Church authorities. In seven places he was brought into court for alleged infractions of the ecclesiastical laws, but only once was he forced to pay a fine. In most cases the opposition only succeeded in making itself look ridiculous while he kept his equanimity and trust in the Lord. On one occasion in court, when the judge was having difficulty defining what "extemporaneous prayer" was, he gave Franson permission to demonstrate prayer in his own words. He prayed in a loud voice, and when he was through, the judge dismissed the case. Eventually, these cases came to the attention of King Oscar, and he ordered the statutes which had been used against the revival preacher cancelled.

When Franson was challenged directly to explain his methods, he did so with zest. "Mr. Franson," a reporter asked, "shouldn't the Holy Spirit be given freedom in meetings to do as He wishes?"

"Yes, Amen, freedom in you and freedom in me," he replied.

"But when you press people to accept Christ, don't you run ahead of the Holy Spirit? He has His time for each soul."

"That is true," said Franson, "but His appointed time is now. When God has been waiting for a soul fifty or sixty years, how can we say that we run ahead of God in dealing with that person?"

"Another question, Mr. Franson, if you please. Don't you feel that your aftermeetings make it very late for people to come home?"

"I don't like late meetings any more than you do," he chuckled, "but, for that matter, compare the aftermeetings of the world. They run late too, but I haven't heard you complain about that!"

"To be frank, Mr. Franson, your work upsets and disturbs the peace of many families."

"Well, yes, and that is entirely scriptural." Mr. Franson looked around at his questioners. "My friends, there are so many objections to the aftermeetings, but Paul said, 'That I might by all means save some.' Aftermeetings meet the need of some people. The ritualistic way is not suitable for all people. Is there not a great distance between the pulpit and the audience? The aim of my aftermeetings is to come close to the individual. It takes discernment. If a preacher has not detected any signs of worry over their lost condition among the people, he should never start an aftermeeting.

"Some people do not believe in quick conversion, but the well-known evangelist, Mr. Moody, says, 'I do not believe in any other.' You wonder why we have results, and again I'll give you the answer Moody did. He said, 'You throw out the net, but I pull it in!' Mr. Moody expected results and got them."

The group around him was silent. They waited for him to continue. "These methods are not the main thing, however. Prayer is the key. That is the way I prepare. Remember that Martin Luther often prayed for three hours on his knees. When a man does that, then he can go out in the power of the Holy Spirit and explain in the simplest, most convincing way what sin is, and judgment, confession, grace, and forgiveness."

Franson tucked his Bible under his arm. "Good night, gentlemen," he said, "I shall not be troubling you much longer. In a few weeks I shall be going to Norway."

Sweden had not yet accepted this earnest servant of the Lord, but Franson would not give up—in the providence of God he would return.

Chapter 12

REVIVAL IN NORWAY

T HE CONDUCTOR SAYS we are stopped only sixty miles from Oslo," Franson told his fellowworker Hallgren.

"So near and yet so far," said Hallgren. "Who would have thought we would be held up by a snowdrift in the mountains and miss our first meeting in Norway?"

Franson looked out the window at the firs blanketed with snow. It was a bitter day in January, 1893. "God knows all about it," he replied, "and I am sure He will make provision in our absence."

He had just had a tramp up and down the railroad tracks, and instead of fretting over the delay, he was thanking the Lord for the beauty of the earth. Now he took out the letter from the Free Mission Society of Norway's capital city inviting them to come. He read again the lines which said, "Great as the need is among the lost, judgment must start in the house of the Lord. We in the free churches need the stirring of the Holy Spirit in our midst to bring us once again to revival power. We believe that you as the Lord's servant can be used to remove apathy and smugness from our hearts."

Several hours later the train began to move slowly forward. It proceeded without further delay to its destination. Franson and Hallgren were met at the station and whisked immediately to the Mission for the afternoon service. "How did you make out this morning, Brother Ostby?" Franson asked in the carriage which took them.

"Oh, all went well. We had a full house as we do this afternoon, and at the last minute someone was able to give a Bible reading in your place."

"Thank you, dear God!" Franson ejaculated.

He had prayed much for guidance as he began his ministry among the Norwegians. Then he chose for this first sermon the Bible account of the raising of Lazarus, using the words of Jesus, "Take ye away the stone."

As he described the stones of factionalism, worldliness, and low standards of Christian living, he could sense the impact on his hearers. "These stones in your lives block the way for the manifestation of Christ's resurrection power," he declared. When he closed his message and opened the meeting for prayer, the Christians responded with a flow of earnest petitions to God to clear these hindrances from their lives.

Revival started, and soon it was difficult to find places large enough for the meetings. The State Church influence sought to thwart Franson wherever possible. When the free church people succeeded in renting a gymnasium, it was only on condition that Franson would not have any raising of hands in the aftermeetings. Because he did not believe that restriction would be a fatal handicap, he agreed. Meanwhile, they kept looking for larger auditoriums. They found a dance hall proprietor who was willing to rent to them, but when the State Church preachers objected, the owner raised his rental to such an exorbitant figure they could not pay it.

The press was hostile but found it could not check this movement of the Spirit. One reporter had sneeringly commented in print that he had attended a meeting. Out of 1700 who were there he estimated that 1400 were "of the lowest class of people in the city." In democratic Norway this supercilious remark turned the tide of public opinion in Franson's favor.

For his part, he ignored the criticism. He was rejoicing in the receptive spirit he found among the Christians. The believers got right with God themselves and then took part in the aftermeetings from the very beginning. Hundreds turned to the Lord, and he had an adequate force of personal workers to deal with the new converts.

Earlier revivals under Hans Nilsen Hauge had produced a strong pietistic laymen's movement which centered around Bible reading and prayer. Those who gathered in cottage prayer meetings were known publicly as "readers." Now the revival under Franson brought this term to the forefront again. Old friends would ask a new convert, "Are you a reader?" And the truly born-again believer would gladly confess, "I am a reader!"

The revival spread ahead of Franson. It had already reached Larvik when he came there, but the Christians were needing leadership in personal work. After he had showed them how to witness for Christ, they demonstrated a zeal he had not experienced elsewhere.

Invited to Arendal by a Pastor Wettergren, he held meetings in a church which held a thousand people. On the first night Franson closed his message as usual with a period of prayer. "I invite you each one to make a short prayer for your own relatives who need to be saved," he said, and what followed was a chorus of prayer, at first by Christians and then by unsaved people who were under conviction. As many as eighty were down on their knees praying for forgiveness at the same time. Above the sound of their prayers Franson could be heard saying, "O Jesus, now these dear ones will not have to weep in hell. They are praying now before Thee, confessing their sins and asking for grace. Oh, forgive them their sins because of Thy precious blood!"

Out of such repentance sprang great relief of heart. Franson wrote to his mother, "The Lord touched the people in a way that could make both body and soul rejoice in the living God. On Sunday there was such a big crowd there had to be two meetings. The church was filled twice, even though Pastor Wettergren spoke to a filled basement at the same time I was preaching upstairs."

On up the coast of Norway Franson went. His team had the same response in Hitteren, where he was allowed to use the State Church hall. In Bergen even though the Methodists and Baptists opened their halls to him, the crowds were too large to handle. He organized a large corps of personal workers to handle the outreach from his meetings. By summer he had to rest for a while in the Opdal valleys and mountains in order to recuperate from the heavy physical and spiritual drain which had been on him. Sometimes he had been called in the middle of the night to get up and pray for people who were wrestling with spiritual decisions, and this physician of souls was not one to lie in bed when such calls came.

Rest for him meant to get away temporarily from people and be alone with God. He came back from Opdal with a renewed spring in his step and joy shining in his face. "I spent many blessed hours with Jesus," he told his friends. "Oh, it was heaven on earth!"

In a great many places Franson helped organize mission churches as a result of his meetings, and his very success in doing this hardened some of the opposition to him. It was one thing when the religious enthusiasts around him met informally, but when they withdrew from the State Church and developed into free churches, they were frowned upon.

The result was that when Franson returned to Alesund for meetings in 1884 with a co-worker, Axel Andersen, hooligans entered the hall to shout and clap their hands. They succeeded in breaking up the meetings, and when the chief of police publicly announced on the third day that he would take no further responsibility to try and maintain order, a howling crowd gathered and drove the evangelists out of town. Franson walked along the stony road, heedless of their taunts. Then he stepped up on an outcropping boulder, turned, and faced them like an Old Testament prophet. They quieted down, and he pronounced a judgment on them. "As you have driven me out of town," he said, "so shall you one day be driven out of this town."

A crestfallen group of young men straggled back into town, and the prophecy was forgotten. Twenty years later, however, when a great conflagration swept the town, the townsfolk did flee out this same road. Then they remembered the way they had treated Franson, and the warning he gave them.

Chapter 13

PHYSICIAN OF SOULS

F<small>RANSON HAD SPENT</small> a year and a half in Sweden, and some thirteen months in Norway. Now he turned his attention to the smallest, and in some ways most indifferent, of the Scandinavian countries, little Denmark. His friends in the mission hall in Oslo were sorry to see him go, because he had taken a special interest in their work. Sensing their need for a more adequate building, he had appealed for funds in Swedish and American church papers. Most of the needed money came in, the plans were drawn, and the new mission house, "Bethlehem," was to be built in a few months.

"You must come back to preach in 'Bethlehem,'" they urged him.

"I hope to do that," he said, "but you also must come to my help. Please pray for the meetings in Denmark. I know I shall be short of the kind of trained helpers I have had here."

When Franson reached Copenhagen in October, 1884, he found no welcome from the evangelical free church leaders. The Inner Mission Society voted against cooperating with him, basing their opposition on the belief that salvation was a process that continued throughout one's whole life. However, Pastor Frans Johnson from Stockholm, who had helped in the free church work in Denmark for fifteen years, sided with Franson. He helped him locate a place for meetings, an English Moravian church, and gradually other halls opened to him in other parts of the city.

For nearly three months Franson preached to a stone wall. It seemed as though Satan had bound the people with chains and would not let them go. Then around Christmas and during the week of prayer at New Year's a gracious break began which widened into a rich harvest. The revival had come, and such a revival as this city had never before seen. Franson wrote to church groups in Sweden and Norway for workers, and several came to his aid.

God now led Franson into a new and unexpected ministry which surprised him as much as it did everyone else. He was called on to pray for a few sick people, and they were healed. The sick began to come in larger and larger numbers until he had to hold special meetings for them. In later years he described what happened as follows: "An experience started such as I had never seen. So many people came, they had to wait for days until we could pray for them, and they waited patiently. Then we decided to pray for three or four at a time, and sometimes seven and eight. All this was done very quietly and before God."

It was the quiet before the storm. Franson was called to preach in other parts of the country, and everywhere he went he was asked to pray for the sick. He could not avoid it, nor would he. But the evangelicals who were most closely identified with him in people's minds made haste to disassociate themselves from him. Pastor Wilhelm Beck, leader of the Inner Mission group, declared, "Mr. Franson can almost perform miracles. It is the world's lot to allow itself to be deceived, but the people of God must keep their heart's door shut against Mr. Franson and his deeds. The time of miracles is past."

Franson did not argue the theology of what was happening. He hadn't asked for it, and he continued to preach for spiritual results. Not everyone who asked him to pray for physical needs was healed. One day a woman with hands badly crippled by arthritis came, and she was not helped.

Shortly thereafter, the woman's husband brought a court case against Franson, saying that he had injured her, and she should have compensation. Under the legal framework in Denmark, Franson could be held by the police during examination of the case. At the hearing Franson was brought from his cell into the courtroom where he faced his accusers. When he was asked for his side of the case, he simply said that he had done nothing, but if his accusers were willing to swear an oath on God's Holy Word regarding this alleged injury, he would pay the required compensation. On the witness stand the woman lost her composure and said she could not give any oath and that she could not remember what had happened. The judge dismissed the case, but Franson remained in custody.

Behind the scenes the ministry of justice was trying to decide what to do with this controversial foreigner. The queen of Sweden was intervening in his behalf, but other influential people in Denmark were equally eager to see him deported. Finally, on Good Friday of 1885, he was released under orders to leave the country. On Easter he went down with friends to the ferry for Malmo, Sweden. On the dock he knelt in prayer and thanked God for all He had done, strange though it was. He then boarded the vessel and left Denmark.

When he discussed the half-year campaign in that country with Christian workers in Stockholm, they had many questions.

"Do you expect to continue your healing ministry in Sweden?" they asked.

"No, not here," he replied. "I believe God had to use something special to wake up the Danish Christians and the unconverted. I would not have chosen to do it, but I did not dare check what God was doing."

"Will you seek to clear your name in any way?"

"I see no point in leaping to my own defense. The hundreds who were truly converted know what God has done for them. The many who were healed will never forget what God has done for them. Even those whom God did not touch physically will testify to spiritual blessing. I am still getting letters from them."

"But do you feel you should leave this legal injustice uncondemned, Brother Franson?"

"If I felt the Lord wanted me to speak out, then I would," Franson answered. "But there is something far more important. I believe God wants us to send more workers back into Denmark to conserve and to carry on the revival there. One or two friends have been preaching in various places such as Thisted and Aalborg, and souls continue to be saved. The main question is, who else will go, and are you willing to send them?"

Shortly thereafter Pastor C. W. Gillen left for Denmark to continue the evangelistic meetings and organize groups of believers. In the space of a few weeks this developed into an association of churches with a paper named the *Morning Star* to represent the movement, and also a foreign missionary society to take the gospel into other parts of the world.

Franson next returned to Oslo for a week's meetings in "Bethlehem," the new mission hall. During the daytime he held courses for evangelists. His instruction to young Christian workers consisted of four parts:

1) How to be so filled with the Holy Spirit that at every meeting souls would be led to the Lord.

2) How to select and use the simplest and most practical Bible texts to convict sinners and backsliders.

3) How to understand the purpose of an aftermeeting, and how to conduct it.

4) How best to counsel inquirers and others in spiritual trouble.

When the day's lectures were over, the students departed, and Franson was alone in his room. He sometimes wished he had a companion with whom he could talk over his own problems and plans. He counseled others, but who would counsel him? Would a wife be the answer?

Friends had tried to joke with him a little about being single. His mother had written after Marie was married suggesting that he was the last of her children to have no home of his own and that it would make her happy if he settled down.

Franson would not reply to this type of hint, but when at last he felt God was speaking to him about marriage, he grew deeply serious. He prayed about it, and then he proposed to a gifted Christian young lady who had assisted him in several meetings. She was not unprepared, for God had been speaking to her too.

She agreed to the engagement; but soon afterward he had to leave for meetings in Germany. The two of them corresponded regularly, writing long letters in which they reported their evangelistic activities. They discussed many subjects on paper and found great delight in their similarity of viewpoint.

Later, however, when Franson met her in Oslo she was obviously troubled.

"Fredrik," she said, "I don't think we made a mistake in getting engaged when we did, but I believe we would make a mistake to get married."

"What do you mean, my dear one?" he cried.

"I believe the Lord gave, but that now He is taking away. We have begun to cherish the thought of life lived together, and I believe the Lord would allow us to have this if we insist on it. But is it best for us or for the work to which God has called us?"

"I don't understand how the Lord could have led us thus far if He doesn't mean us to work together," he muttered.

"I don't understand it either," she replied, tears filling her eyes, "but somehow I feel God wants you to remain free to do His bidding, to move here and there, and to have Christ as your first and only allegiance."

"And you? What of you? Are you willing for this sacrifice?"

She looked into his eyes. "Yes. The Lord has made me willing," she said.

There was a long silence. Then Franson replied, "I must accept your decision, but God has not yet made me willing to give up the hope that you will be mine. How will this change our relationship? May I still write to you?"

"Yes, Fredrik," she said. "Let us still be friends. Let us trust God."

Months later Franson wrote from Germany, "I can accept my disappointment now. The Lord has let the blessings roll in and all the hurt go out."

Chapter 14

A DREAM FULFILLED

T HE YEAR 1885 had run half its course. Franson jostled through the crowds of students in the quaint university city of Bonn, his Bible and notebook under his arm. He was in a hurry to reach the lecture room of Professor Christlieb who taught theology. The baron who had opened his home to Franson had highly recommended this Christian scholar.

He was early and able to get a good seat. He listened attentively to the chatter of students around him, trying to catch as much as possible of their swift flow of German. Following Christlieb was easier because he spoke slowly and clearly. Franson's pen raced as he kept notes. Here was a professor who did not agree with the rampant higher criticism of the day and was willing to say so. "Evil is an organized realm," he said, "and the Bible teaches that it is ruled over by a personal devil. One reason why sin is so terrible is that even a little contact with sin puts you in contact with this well-organized realm and its ruler."

Franson felt like uttering a loud amen, but he restrained himself. His heart was glad that God had given him these weeks in Bonn, where he could plunge into renewed study of German and put aside some of the thoughts which would otherwise fill his mind. He was determined to improve his spoken German to the place where he could preach without an interpreter. Before long, he was preaching every evening, giving simple Bible studies. This continued for two months. When it came time to leave the city, he went down to the railway station and bought a fourth-class ticket to Barmen. A friend who had accompanied him expostulated with him. "What would the baron think if he knew you traveled this way? Why do you go fourth class?"

"I go fourth class because there is no fifth class," Franson replied calmly. His evangelistic work took him from place to place—Eberfeld, Solingen, Essen, Mulhein, Strassburg, and Stuttgart. A new gentleness began to appear in his preaching, though he had never been one to criticize or even mention his opponents and the State Church.

In children's meetings he would ask, "How many of you love Jesus? Will you put up your hands?"

Then he would say, "I see that some of you don't seem to be sure. Let me tell you how Jesus took the little ones into His arms and blessed them, and perhaps carried them on His shoulders! Come here, close to me, and I'll tell you."

Then the children gathered around and listened raptly as he told them Bible stories. Afterward he prayed for them and blessed them, often putting his hands on their heads. They were not likely to forget this man of God who could make Bible characters and truths so attractive.

In one aftermeeting he approached a grouchy sergeant who struck him so hard that the Bible fell out of his hand. Franson picked up the Bible and held it out toward the soldier, saying, "According to the words of this Book, you are forgiven."

He then went on about his work of dealing with others

in the hall. Before long the soldier got up and went out, but on his way home he was convicted of sin. He knelt down on the street and asked God to take pity on him. The next night he was back to shake Franson warmly by the hand and beg his forgiveness.

Franson continually looked past the exteriors of men to their inner struggles, and was eager for them to find deliverance and help in God. Therefore, if anyone was criticized in his presence, he was apt to change the subject or say, "Yes, yes, let us pray."

Once a fellow worker remarked in exasperation, "Schmidt surely has a screw loose!"

Franson countered by saying, "Everybody has a screw loose, and I have two loose ones!"

Although he was particularly mindful of students and wished to reach every university center in Germany, he never neglected other opportunities, even with the most simple. Passing a blacksmith, he asked him if he was saved. The man gaped at him, not knowing what to answer. "Get down on your knees," Franson ordered. The tall, grizzled man looked with amazement at the slight figure before him and then lowered his hefty frame to the ground.

"Now pray to God," Franson continued.

"Dear God," panted the blacksmith, "save me from this here man because he is crazy!"

"Amen!" exclaimed Franson in delight and clapped his hands together. "Get up, my friend, get up! I didn't mean to scare you, but I see that you have the fear of the Lord in your heart. Yes, you're right. In the eyes of some, I may be sort of crazy, but the Lord can use even fools to serve Him."

Into this round of meetings and personal work God

brought an unexpected fulfillment of Franson's long-standing desire to tour southern Europe. He received an anonymous gift specified for travel through Europe and to the Holy Land.

For years Franson had been trusting the Lord alone to meet his needs, even though Moody Church had offered more than once to provide for him as one of their missionaries. He believed that as long as he was willing for the "ravens" to feed him, this would release the funds in Chicago to care for some other Christian worker.

When this large gift for travel reached him, he was at first uncertain whether he should use it, but he decided that, like Paul, he should be willing to abound as well as to be abased. He turned his steps southward with the confidence that the Lord was going before him.

Switzerland, with its Alps and shimmering lakes, where Zwingli and Calvin lived and ministered, southern France with its Huguenot assemblies, northern Italy with its small groups of Waldensians— to Franson this was a tour of church history. When he arrived in Rome, he exclaimed, "This is holy ground!" not because it was the seat of the pope but because of the thousands of Christian martyrs who were slain there. Like many other tourists he visited the Colosseum and the catacombs. Farther south he stopped in Naples and went to see the ruins of Pompeii.

Writing home, he said, "I have seen the way these Romans lived, ate, drank, worked, and worshiped, and the terrible wickedness that prevailed in this city before sudden destruction came upon it. Now it all lies open and exposed to the glare of daylight. What a reminder it is to me of the day when everything we have done in this life will be uncovered unless we repent and are cleansed by the blood of Jesus Christ!"

Next Franson took ship to Alexandria in Egypt, visiting Cairo and the Pyramids. From there his ship took him to Jaffa. Disembarking, he rode by horseback the fifty-three miles through the Palestinian hills to Jerusalem. His first Sunday there, he attended English and German services. He met a group of elderly Americans who called themselves "Overcomers." They had come from Chicago and now devoted themselves to ministering to the Arabs. When Franson urged them to learn Arabic in order to communicate with the people of the land, they demurred, saying, "No, our deeds of mercy will speak for us and for the Lord."

During the twenty-three days he spent in the Holy Land, almost half the time was given to meetings. He missed seeing Mount Carmel in order to speak to a group of Germans in Haifa. Nevertheless, he saw a great many points of interest. He was disappointed by the commercialization and ostentatious displays in the shrines. The quieter places were more rewarding.

At Emmaus, when monks showed him the place where Jesus was supposed to have broken bread on the first Easter, Franson told them the story of his own conversion and had a time of prayer with them. On Mount Gerizim he found a community of Samaritans who still carried on their ancient worship and venerated an old manuscript of the Pentateuch. Even though they were worshiping in ignorance, they carried a more genuine link with the past than anything else he had seen. When he reached Jacob's well, where Jesus had asked the Samaritan woman for a drink, and spoke to her of living water, he found it dry. "Well," he said, "I'm glad that I am not trusting in this well but in the Water of Life!"

Then heading northward into Syria, Franson visited the

American College at Beirut. The president, Dr. Daniel Bliss, arranged for him to speak to the students.

"I have just traveled through a good part of the Near East," he said. "And while I can't speak your native language, there is one word I have learned very well. I have heard it almost daily. Do you wonder what it is? It is the word *baksheesh*."

The students tittered. They all knew how tourists were plagued with this cry for a handout.

"I didn't like this word at all," he continued, "and once I actually tried to pay my guides not to say it. But they couldn't restrain themselves. Out it came, 'Baksheesh, baksheesh!' It was such a habit with them. Then in one of my meetings, I was speaking about the Gift of God, and the translator used this word *baksheesh*. You know, from that time on, I have had a different view of the word, I just wish each one of you were crying out to God for His 'baksheesh,' the Lord Jesus Christ."

Most of the students were Muslims, but they listened raptly to Franson's presentation of the gospel. When he finished, some of them hurried to Dr. Bliss and asked him to have this man speak again. Thus began a revival such as the college had never before witnessed, with several accepting Christ as Saviour and the rest visibly impressed.

* * *

Patmos, Smyrna, Constantinople, Odessa—on Franson moved, speaking to Armenians, Turks, and Russians as doors opened for him. He had no fixed schedule. He was only concerned about reaching men for Christ. He came back through Poland and Prussia, tanned and relaxed and ready for his evangelistic work once again.

Chapter 15

FIFTY FOR CHINA

THE CONVICTION was now growing on Franson that he could multiply his usefulness by training evangelists to go out into the country districts of Norway and Sweden and then over the Baltic to Germany. He had already experimented with courses patterned after those taught by Moody, and he believed these were the answer to the present need in Scandinavia.

He went back to Oslo for six months in 1888 and found a warmth of welcome and an interest in the Bible that encouraged him. People were keenly interested in religious matters. The gospel was table talk even for the unconverted. "This is the day of opportunity," he declared. "We must take advantage of it."

The evangelistic courses drew from twenty to eighty students at a time. The arrangements were simple, and the fare plain. In his announcements Franson made it clear that the emphasis would be on sacrifice and self-denial. All he asked of participants was that they have faith in God and high standards of Christian conduct. They must be recommended by some congregation or by individual Christians.

His motto for the students was "Look to Jesus," and he placed much stress on thoroughgoing fellowship with the

Lord. If a Bible class began to drag, he was apt to stop, look around, and then say, "Down on your knees. Let us pray for the Lord to stir us up to attention and love of His Word."

In the long morning sessions such breaks were not unusual. The classes began at nine in the morning and continued for four or five hours. Franson always had his Greek New Testament with him and would refer to it in explaining certain texts. In a typical course he would move speedily through a large number of books of the Bible. He invited discussion and was always very generous with those who disagreed with him. He often said of these courses that no particular sectarian view would be forced on the students, and he took care not to press his own opinions.

He did not expect these courses to give the students more than an introduction to methods of Bible study, but he did count on the time together being an opportunity for the fire of God to enter their souls. For this reason he gave much time to group prayer.

In the afternoons the students went out two by two for house-to-house visitation and personal work. In the evenings they helped in the evangelistic meetings which Franson conducted.

When the graduates of these courses began to move out across the countryside with their accordions and guitars, they created a new and holy ferment with their joy and zeal.

"Sometimes I feel a little bit like I am running a few steps ahead of a train," Franson confided to a friend. "I am getting requests from many places in Sweden and also Finland for the evangelists' courses. There is no way of stopping or standing still."

It was prayer that set so much in motion, and he was always willing to stop for this. Seeing one of the young evangelists off on his way home, Franson walked along with him and then suggested a time of prayer by the roadside. When they had prayed for two hours, the young man timidly ventured to say, "Mr. Franson, perhaps you had better return now, as your hostess may be waiting dinner for you."

"I would rather go on and pray for two more hours," Franson replied, "because when a person has been praying for a while, he doesn't want to do anything else but pray."

His companion gulped, and Franson relented. "However, I'm sure it is time for you to be on your way and for me to get back to my meal. Good-bye now, and God bless you." Prayer was very dear to him, and he found it hard to understand when others did not take equal delight in it.

When Franson was a house guest, he kept very much to himself and did not intrude on the activities of the household. He visited with his host at mealtimes, but betweentimes stayed much in his room. He did not expect others to follow his routine in prayer, but he found it most necessary.

Leaving Norway, he now went back to Sweden to teach more training courses. On the train in one place he entered a compartment, tucked his small bag under the seat, and sat down with his Bible on his lap. As the train pulled out of the station, he looked around at his fellowpassengers. "I wonder how many of you believe in God and want to live in fellowship with Him," he said. Several nodded or motioned their assent. "Well, then, let us use the time we have together on this trip to pray," he proposed.

At this, some passengers got to their feet and fled to the next compartment. The rest got down on their knees with Franson for a hearty prayer meeting. After prayer, they listened to him expound God's Word, and the informal meeting continued until they reached the next station.

Later Franson went to Finland to conduct a Bible course, and fifty or sixty people gathered in a Helsinki church. Some of his students were preachers and university professors. One meeting he held in the Alliance House was attended by a bishop and many of the intelligentsia of the city. When Franson gave the invitation, about one hundred and fifty students went to the inquiry room, and many of them were saved. From this number he found those who were eager to witness for Christ, even in foreign lands.

As he met with those who were serious about Christian service, he had a new challenge to lay before them.

"We live in unusual days," he said. "More is done nowadays in one year than formerly was done in ten years. To every ten missionaries who formerly went out on the mission field, one hundred now go. Sons and daughters from wealthy English and American families step down from their noble rank and leave their possessions to follow the lowly Nazarene in His steps. They offer themselves on God's altar to live frugally and to dress plainly. They are saying, 'Lord, what will You have us to do? Do whatever You desire with us, even if we lose our good name.' They are willing to be considered visionary and fanatic because they go out to the ends of the earth for the sake of Christ. Are you willing to do the same?"

God had been preparing the ground for this message. Three years before, a young Finnish student had spent the winter in London. While there he had become acquainted with Hudson Taylor and the China Inland Mission. Antti Makinen had been greatly moved by what he had seen and heard, and on his return to Finland he had told others about this mission which operated solely by faith. Now he gave his report again.

Franson listened with keen interest. "You Finns should do the same thing here," he said. "Surely God can move upon hearts to go to the mission field and also provide all their needs as you pray and believe."

They raised a fund of a thousand markkar as a beginning, and Agnes Meyer, who was called to China during Franson's meetings, was the first to go.

Something new was stirring in Franson's mind and heart as he went back to Sweden and then down to Germany. He explained it to his evangelistic team in Berlin. Emanuel Olson and the Wettergren brothers were with him. "The Lord is leading in the saving of many souls," he said, "and from among these new converts we find many with a great desire to serve their Saviour. You know, I train them in evangelists' courses to go out in the highways and byways to witness for Christ. But this is not all. They are beginning to go overseas. We have nine such workers here in Germany now. Others have gone to Denmark. It cannot stop here. What of those who wish to go to China and other mission fields? How will they go out? I have had many young people ask me this, and I am sure God will do something about it."

In 1890 Nellie Hall, Ida Nihlen, Ninnie Akeson, and Emil Jacobson had joined him in Berlin, and the work there stepped up in intensity. These mission workers felt they were missionaries in a needy field. The land of Luther had lost much of its evangelicalism and needed the gospel. Franson had selected Berlin as the hardest and most anti-

Christian city in Germany. God blessed the work there. Then they fanned out to Linden, Siegen, Göttingen, Elberfeld, and Barmen. In each of the last two places Franson held a ten-day series of meetings and had fifteen to twenty come forward every evening to receive Christ.

In Barmen he organized a mission society of two-hundred members. It was at this point that he heard of Hudson Taylor's appeal for one thousand new missionaries for China. Taylor was not asking that all of these be members of the China Inland Mission. He was calling on all Christians of all churches to respond to the need of China's millions.

The believers in Barmen went to prayer about this. "Oh God," cried Franson, "give us a part in giving the gospel to China."

Emanuel Olson was the first answer to that prayer when he rose to his feet and stated that, although he had been planning to go to Africa as a missionary, now he believed God wanted him to be a missionary among the Chinese. Several others volunteered, and a new missionary movement was underway.

Those were unusually busy days. Franson hastily organized the German Alliance Mission and corresponded with the China Inland Mission about cooperating with them. When he received word that the new candidates could go to London for training and then proceed to China as associates of the CIM, he did everything he could to speed them on their way. The welcome news came that he had received an inheritance, and without hesitation he contributed this to the outgoing of the first party. He planned to escort the ten recruits as far as England.

When all preparations were complete, the Barmen mission had a day of fasting and prayer. Then that evening the leaders commissioned Emanuel Olson and the other nine with the laying on of hands. Franson poured out his heart for these young people and for the Chinese who would hear the gospel for the first time through their ministry. "O dear Father," he said, "Thou hast given these ten; give us more. Give us at least fifty from Germany for the land of China!"

Chapter 16

GIVE ME MEN FOR MISSIONS

PASSENGERS WERE OUT ON DECK EARLY as the ship slipped
through the quiet waters of lower New York harbor.
"There she is," someone called, and all eyes followed the
pointing finger. The Statue of Liberty was looming in
sight. For Fredrik Franson and many others it was the
first they had seen the famous monument on Bedloe's
Island. It had been erected during Franson's nine years'
absence.

He had thrilled when he read in newspapers the poetry
of Emma Lazarus, champion of Jewish immigrants from
Russia, to whom this symbol seemed to say:

> Give me your tired, your poor,
> Your huddled masses yearning to breathe free,
> The wretched refuse of your teeming shore.
> Send these, the homeless, tempest-tossed to me,
> I lift my lamp beside the golden door!

To Franson, leaning on the rail, the lifted torch spoke
of the light of the gospel, the firmly grasped tablet was
the Word of God, the figure not stationary but a missionary going out from these shores, carrying the message of
liberty to countless millions in darkness.

It was a September Sunday in 1890, and he knew he
had meetings scheduled that very day at the Swedish

Pilgrim Church in Brooklyn and in other churches of the city. He was feeling fit again after some miserable days at sea. He nodded to a fellow passenger. "It's wonderful not to be rolling anymore," he said.

"I guess you were pretty sick," his friend replied.

"Yes," said Franson. "I think seasickness is the only sickness the Lord doesn't heal. He certainly doesn't hear me when I ask Him to deliver me from it. I remember making a trip on the Baltic. I was reading in the Psalms where it says, 'Let the sea roar . . . let the floods clap their hands.' I groaned. 'Oh Lord,' I prayed, 'don't let them clap too loudly,' but we sailed right into a storm!"

They laughed, and turned their attention to the Manhattan shoreline.

Franson had left America early in his career. Now at 38 he was at the height of his physical strength and a spiritual dynamo as well. He was ready when friends met him at the pier and rushed him off to four services that first day. For the next six weeks he preached daily to packed churches up and down the east coast. As a result of these contacts he had fifty young men and women on hand when he opened a Bible and missionary course in Brooklyn. It was October 14, 1890, and he was setting in motion a missionary movement in America which was going to involve him far more than he realized.

"Are you failing to yield to what God wants you to do?" he appealed to the young people. "Some men and women have their souls saved, but their unyielded lives are lost. They are wasted with no fruit for eternity.

"We have the power to live and serve Jesus Christ. It is not our power. The source is with Him, and it is the greatest source of power there is. Remember, the higher the source, the greater the pressure. If the Lord is the

Source of our life, the pressure will be on us to reach out. It is a pressure that will send us to the ends of the earth with the gospel."

He swung into his practical instructions to evangelists. "Some of you will be working in the home fields," he said. "Some of you will be going to China, God willing. Where-ever you are, when you give a testimony or when you preach, use illustrations. If you can hang truth on the hook of a story, it will help you become fishers of men.

"And when you pray, my young friends, don't offer dry prayers to God. He doesn't want prayers that are so pious they tell Him a hundred things He knew before you were born. Please, let's not have any more slipshod repetition of religious phrases that have lost their meaning.

"But prayer is marvelous when you mix faith with it, faith for others and faith for yourself. Sometimes when you have been working hard all day, you will find it hard to speak in the evening. You will need to pray to God for strength to keep on. And then often you will need to pray for grace to relax. After I have been in a revival meeting followed by a long, blessed aftermeeting, I find it difficult to go to sleep. When I try to go to sleep, everything I have to do tomorrow, or the next day, and the next day, comes to my mind. I realize it is the devil who is trying to keep me from sleeping by telling me what I'm going to do. I've found out how to meet him. As soon as he begins to remind me of what I have to do, I ask the Lord to take care of it. Then when the devil reminds me of something else, I say, 'Lord, now You must take care of that also.' And when the devil finds that all he can do by reminding me of things is to get me to pray, he gives up and tries to lull me to sleep instead!"

So it went, and by the end of the course, twenty of

the young people were selected for missionary service in China. Franson had presented the overwhelming need of that land and they felt called to go.

They came from different denominations, and thus he visualized for them an alliance mission. They were to go out and serve as associates of the China Inland Mission for three years. After that they would be free to join the mission of their choice.

"I shall give other courses in Chicago and Minneapolis," he told them. "I'll keep in touch with you, and we'll meet somewhere west of there. Go on home now to say good-bye to your loved ones, and let's keep believing for the Lord's supply for your outgoing."

In Chicago, Franson quickly got in touch with Professor Fridolf Risberg with whom he had worked in Sweden, Rev. August Pohl, Rev. C. T. Dyrness, and other friends. "I need a committee to handle the funds which are coming in," he said. "We shall have to have some type of organization."

These men warmed to his vision and agreed to act as the board. They decided to call it the China Alliance Mission and appeal to Christian people to back up the missionary volunteers and send them out. Thus, on October 14, 1890, that which is today The Evangelical Alliance Mission came into being.

"What are your requirements for candidates?" the board asked Franson.

"I regard as basic that the candidate be born-again, that he has won a soul to Christ, that he has some practical talent, such as the ability to play a musical instrument, and that he is willing to suffer for Christ."

"What about health and education?"

"We want people with sound bodies and keen intelligence, but the most important thing is their spiritual maturity and stability. I have seen again and again in the old country that higher education was not necessarily the key to success in evangelism. They will have lots of studying to do when they learn the Chinese language."

Brother Pohl asked, "How much will it take to support a missionary for a year in China?"

Franson had an answer for that. "Emanuel Olson has written about living expenses, and two hundred dollars is sufficient to live simply in the interior for twelve months."

Risberg, acting as secretary, took notes. Pohl agreed to be treasurer. Then they got down on their knees and committed the future into God's hands.

The Chicago Bible and evangelism course was a grinding six hours of lectures daily for eleven days, but Franson seemed to thrive in the midst of the seventy promising young people who enrolled. At the close of the course about thirty of them were on the platform of the Swedish Mission Covenant Tabernacle to sing, play their guitars, and tell of their call to China.

Then Franson rose and said, "Thousands of Chinese villages are without a single witness. Hudson Taylor is calling for a thousand new missionaries to go to these villages. God is calling on America to help send them out. You have been sitting here, your hearts thrilled by these testimonies and lifted into heavenly places with the singing. You are well fed with spiritual blessings, while the heathen go hungry. These young people are ready to do all they can. They are willing to go. What will you do to speed them on their way?"

His messages in Swedish, Norwegian, and English-speaking churches around Chicago pressed on the tender consciences of Christians. They were seeing spiritual realities as never before. In private he was equally insistent. Finding Dyrness in his study at Salem Church, he said to him, "Brother, I believe your church should take on the support of two of these candidates for China."

"Support two missionaries?" Dyrness said incredulously. "Our deacons were thinking of taking up a special offering."

"How far would that go?" Franson replied. "No, I think you should set your sights higher. If you'll trust God, He'll make it possible."

"But we have only thirty-four members, and they are not rich," Dyrness objected.

"Pastor Dyrness," Franson said, "you've got a rich God. I'm sure this is God's will for your church. We must get these two out to China this winter."

Dyrness wrestled with the question for several days. He thought of the present obligations of the small congregation. He imagined the objections of the church board if he should make such a proposal. Then he realized that he was not arguing with Franson but with God. God wanted this step of faith.

That Sunday he preached with new power. After the service he called a meeting of the deacons and presented the matter, and they immediately voted to take on the support of the two missionaries.

Franson moved on to Minneapolis for a course, and then to Omaha. Here many of the candidates from the other courses joined him, expecting to be commissioned and to go on to China. They met in the Swedish Mission Church whose pastor, the Rev. J. A. Hultman, was called the "Sunshine Singer." Melody filled the air. The Christmas decorations in the church auditorium added a festive touch, but it was a solemn sight when the first thirty-five out of a group of seventy were commissioned. They knelt at the front and were consecrated by prayer and the laying on of hands.

About six o'clock in the winter evening of the following day, the whole group marched in a body to the Union Pacific station, led by Franson and Hultman. Carrying their bags and guitars, they sang as they walked along. Bystanders gawked in amazement, asking, "Who are they? Immigrants?"

Someone laughed and said, "They're emigrating to the celestial kingdom."

"Yes, they're a bunch of Scandinavians going out to convert the Chinese," another said.

Some men staggered out of a saloon, bottles in hand, to see what the excitement was. "Glory, glory, hallelujah!" they shouted off-key, and much amused with themselves. "Glory, glory, hallelujah! His truth is marching on!"

Franson turned around to his band of missionaries. "This is a sign of victory," he exclaimed. "Even our enemies have to sing for the Lord's soldiers."

They moved on. Franson saw one of the young men struggling with a cumbersome, oversize suitcase which he had finally shifted to his shoulder. "Here, let me help you," he ordered, and from there to the station they carried it together.

The group broke into an old favorite:

Oh, brother, when the way seems bleak and long,
Just march on singing;
Mind that the devil flees your hardy song,
While Jesus from on high is praying.

"Crazy Swedes!" commented the uncomprehending, but heaven looked at them from a different viewpoint. Fifteen of this party of thirty-five would lay down their lives in China—one within a few months of arrival, others after years of service, some stricken by virulent diseases, others murdered in violence. The way would not be easy, but they went singing.

Franson, knowing that theirs would be a costly road, still urged them on. "Go," he said, "and God will go with you."

Those that were left behind continued under his instruction. A medical doctor named Holmquist had been giving the candidates first-aid instruction, and he continued his lectures too. Twelve days after the first group left, Franson had a second party of fifteen ready to go. The two groups, totaling fifty, arrived in Shanghai three weeks apart. They were the largest number of missionary recruits ever to have reached China as a contingent.

Chapter 17

MORE FIELDS TO HARVEST

ON THEIR WAY TO THE FIELD the two missionary parties
had passed through Japan, and there they saw heathen
worship for the first time. Their letters to Franson about
the need in Japan as well as his contact with some Japanese on the west coast convinced him that God was speaking about other fields besides China. He scheduled three
more Bible and missionary courses in Seattle, Denver, and
Phelps Center, Nebraska, then added another at Des
Moines, Iowa. Through these courses he began to present
the claims of Japan to prospective candidates.

His students often learned valuable lessons just by ob-
serving him and his reactions. While in Denver he was
teaching the Bible one afternoon when he was handed a
telegram. He glanced at it, and his expression changed.
He looked up and said, "My friend, Oscar Noreen, in Kan-
sas, has been called home. Let us pray."

Everyone knelt down, and there was silence for a few
moments. Then he prayed, asking God to comfort the
family. "And, O Lord," he continued, "I wonder if it is
permissible to greet Noreen. O God, if it is not against
Thy divine law, greet him for us. For Jesus' sake. Amen."

After the courses were completed, Franson had fifteen
young people ready to go as missionaries to Japan. The

Mission in Chicago then decided to change its name to The Scandinavian Alliance Mission to provide for its wider scope. Franson traversed the country looking for additional supporters to back the expanding program.

One day a pastor was taking him around in a horse and buggy to show him the sights of his city. They came to the bank of a river and stopped for a while. The pastor's gaze turned toward the buildings on the far side. Prominent among them was a new Civil War Memorial Hall. The pastor said to Franson, "See that beautiful building there with a copper roof that is shining like gold?"

"Yes, yes," he said, but he wasn't looking in that direction.

"It's over this way!"

"Yes, yes." He still wasn't looking.

"It's really a beautiful new building," the pastor tried again.

"Yes, brother," Franson replied. "Don't you think your church could take on the support of another missionary?"

With this kind of faith in action the fifteen sailed for Yokohama in November, 1891. They were followed by another party numbering twelve who sailed for China, in February, 1892. And twelve sailed for India in March of the same year. Franson took special pleasure in the fact that John Fredrickson, his former co-worker in the Midwest and in Utah, was the leader of the India party.

God had sent in twenty-five thousand dollars during the first year of the new mission, but there had been many occasions when the directors were down on their knees in urgent prayer. In spite of this, Franson was undeterred by worries and kept on looking for new fields to enter. When two Chicago Theological Seminary students, Carl Paulsen and Paul Gullander, approached him about work

in Africa, he encouraged them to press on with their
vision.

At this time Franson announced meetings at the Oak
Street Church in Chicago. These were evangelistic, and he
noted the effectiveness with which a young lady named
Miss Moe was helping with the unconverted in the aftermeetings. He approached her at the end of a meeting with
the abrupt assertion, "God wants you to be a missionary
in Africa."

He waited a few nights and then brought up the subject
again. He told her several other young people were interested in going, and that he was planning some training
classes. She thought she would prefer to go to school first.

"God says, 'Go,' and the heathen say, 'Come.' You must
go *now*," he declared.

"But I have a younger sister for whom I am responsible. Perhaps."

"Very well, I'll not talk to you anymore about it. I'm
going home now, and I shall pray that God will send
you." And he left.

Later when God spoke to Malla Moe about going to
Africa, it was as though a great hand pushed her to the
floor. And yet when she went to tell Franson of her change
of mind, he took it very much for granted as though he
had been expecting it all along.

His course with the candidates for Africa lasted only
two weeks. He never asked how much education they
had. He wanted to know if they had been filled with the
Spirit, and if they knew how to trust God. His last advice
to them was, "Fast and pray! If you are sick, fast and
pray. If the language is hard to learn, fast and pray. If
the people will not hear you, fast and pray."

Of the eight, Malla Moe seemed the least prepossessing. When her turn came at the commissioning service in New York City's Bethesda Church, she fumbled. "Now what shall I say?" she asked. "It is not easy to talk to so many people—people of God like this. In the street I said to God, 'God, you give me something to say. You know I know nothing.' He did give me, 'The Lord is my shepherd, I shall not want.' That's all. Amen."

She sat down, and Franson, who was a shrewd judge of character, did not seem fazed. "She'll do," he murmured. "She'll do."

Chapter 18

A HIGH MOUNTAIN AND
DEEP VALLEY

NINETY-SEVEN YOUNG PEOPLE had sailed for the four fields of The Scandinavian Alliance Mission in little over a year. They were commissioned to be itinerant evangelists in places where the gospel had never been preached, and the burden was on them to reach as many people as possible.

When skeptics asked how thorough a work could be done by street preaching and extensive touring, Franson admitted that it was not ideal. "We are up against the problem of a scant number of workers who will be scattered among millions. For those who criticize giving out the gospel and then passing on to the next town, I will merely say that I agree with Mr. Taylor. It is he who said, 'If one offer of the gospel is insufficient, what shall we think of none?'"

Franson had the faith to see beyond pioneering days to the growth of small and then larger churches with national Christian brethren who would join in the work of evangelizing their own people.

As Franson dwelt on the vast unevangelized areas around the world and the enthusiasm with which young Christians were volunteering to serve in them, he wished he had limitless means at his disposal. In little over a year, ninety-seven had been sent to China, Japan, India, and Africa. Now he was receiving letters in large numbers from young people in Scandinavia, begging him to help them get to the fields. He mentioned their needs in the Chicago church papers:

> Only a few days ago I read in a newspaper of two Germans who discovered a gold mine in Colorado, and how they have in a short time obtained one million dollars each from it. I could not help but take the matter to God and ask Him if He could not give us such a mine. Just think what we could do with only one million dollars! It would be enough to support five hundred missionaries for ten years, and we would not need to count the interest.

Some while later, when he was visiting in Cripple Creek, Colorado, some Christian men brought up his own idea to him. "Why, W. F. Stratton came here to Cripple Creek as a poor prospector," they said, "and he discovered the Isabella Mine. He sold it to a British syndicate. Do you know how much he received? Eleven million dollars! Mr. Franson, couldn't we ask God to give us a gold mine for missions?"

"Wouldn't it be wonderful if God would do that?" he mused. "He could, you know. If we had a bucket of gold to dip from, we would escape the worry about support for the missionaries. And we could send out more and more."

"Oh, let's try," they suggested. "We'll go out and prospect for a day, and you pray that God will lead us to a vein of gold."

Franson was never one to dodge a test. To him, faith

was a principle to practice. "Will you go?" he asked. "Then I'll stay home and pray all day. I'll lock myself in a room. You go out, and I'll pray."

They went out early in the morning. Franson spent the whole day fasting and praying in his room. The three men who had gone out prospecting came back after dark. They hadn't found anything, and they were so crestfallen, they sneaked in the back way. Franson heard their voices in the kitchen and came rushing out. "Did you find any gold?" he asked.

"No, Mr. Franson," they replied, most discouraged.

"Well, don't feel let down," he quickly told them. "We'll just learn what God has to teach us in this, and all will be well."

He turned and went back to his room where he had kept his vigil. He had worked that day every bit as hard as they. They trooped along behind, wondering what he would do next.

He knelt down by the cane-bottomed chair and clasped his hands together. "O God, I believe that I understand now," he prayed. "If Thou hadst given us a gold mine then we would have trusted in that gold mine. We wouldn't have seen the necessity of faith. Peter says faith is more precious than gold. So I see now, Thou dost not want us to have a gold mine because Thou wouldst rather give us faith."

His faith was soon to be severely tested. Franson had met Dr. A. B. Simpson when he first arrived in New York City, and his path again crossed that of this great missionary leader at a conference in Omaha. When Simpson announced that funds for missionary work in the Christian and Missionary Alliance were running far ahead of recruits, Franson pricked up his ears. He asked Simpson

for a chance to talk with him and told him about the volunteers in Europe who longed to serve on the mission
fields. "I would be willing to go back there and get two
hundred new missionaries if you would be willing to un-
derwrite their support," he offered.

Simpson weighed this new possibility. He was himself
second to none in missionary passion. "I'm in favor of anything that will send the gospel to the ends of the earth,"
he declared. "I'll take your proposal up with the board
back at the Tabernacle in New York and let you know
our decision."

Good as his word, Simpson soon wrote back to say that
the people at the Tabernacle were enthusiastic about
helping the Scandinavians and had immediately contributed some substantial gifts for this purpose. He invited
Franson to come to New York and discuss arrangements
with the board there. When they met together, they decided that groups of candidates going out at any one
time should be limited to twenty. They would go first to
England to study English for a while and then proceed
to America to meet with Dr. Simpson. After that they
would go on to the mission fields.

The good friends in New York had no conception of
the whirlwind way Franson would start parties of young
missionaries coming their way. He reached Sweden in
August, 1892, and by Christmas he had held four training
courses in the largest cities. Within a year he could report that he had reached his goal of two hundred, forty-
five of whom had already been sent to China. The one
hundred and fifty who remained were ready and waiting
to go.

At this point the blow fell. The Missionary Alliance in
New York voted to accept no more of the Swedish work-

ers. "Yes, there was some talk of two hundred, but no one expected them so fast," they explained. Moreover, some of the American missionaries of the Alliance were objecting strenuously to their new Swedish fellowworkers.

The criticisms emphasized that they were uneducated and untried, but these were not the crucial problems. These European workers had a language barrier that tended to isolate them from the Americans of the Simpson Mission. Added to this was the sensitivity the Americans felt over their own higher salaries. They were embarrassed by the plain way in which these new missionaries lived. Moreover, both America and Europe were heading into a great depression that was throwing a scare even into Christian organizations.

What grieved Franson was that the young missionaries were being criticized by the very missionaries who should have been rejoicing in reinforcements. He found this incomprehensible. He reached for his pen and wrote:

> When I hear the evil report that is being circulated concerning China and the two hundred Swedes who were ready to help take that land for Christ, I have been ready to pray with Samson, "O Lord God, remember me, I pray thee, and strengthen me, I pray thee, only this once, O God, that I may be at once avenged of the Philistines for my two eyes."
>
> The two eyes are in this case the two hundred Swedes. And I do wish that I had the strength of Samson to take hold of the two pillars—bad repute and unbelief—upon which the house of the critics stands, and hurl them to the ground. How can I wish differently, when every mail brings me news from one or another of the Swedish workers saying that opportunities to reach multitudes are presenting themselves everywhere?

For some months Franson held together about a hundred of the candidates while they studied English and also had classes in Chinese. Meanwhile, a torrent of abuse mounted in Sweden, where Franson was now blamed for stirring up groundless hopes and excitement for nothing. Financial conditions worsened, but still he managed to send out nineteen more to China. The others had to go back to their homes. They were disappointed but not disaffected. They would never forget his calm in the midst of the storm or the evidences of God's care for them while they had waited.

Chapter 19

ALL MY SPRINGS ARE IN THEE

F RANSON'S FRIENDS would remember and retell the story
of how they had wanted to give Franson a new suit. The
one he was wearing was frayed and shiny.

"Won't you go to the tailor to be measured?" they
asked him.

"No, I have no time," he replied.

Then one night after he had gone to sleep, a friend
tiptoed into his room, lifted his clothes from the back of
a chair, and took them out. The tailor had come there to
measure them. Later, the new suit was surreptitiously ex-
changed for the old one, again while he slept. The next
morning he dressed, completely unaware that he was
wearing a new suit. Finally, he started to rummage
around for something which had been replaced in the
wrong pocket and discovered what had happened.

❋ ❋ ❋

Franson's correspondence had greatly increased because of the large number of missionaries and supporters
of missionary work who kept in touch with him personally.
Often the mail was a joy, but these months also brought
much distressing news. The Scandinavian Alliance Mission had sent out a party of eight men and four women
to East Africa in 1893. Their ship put in at the British

port of Mombasa, and it seemed as though the long sea voyage would be successfully completed. Then as they went along the coast toward Lamu a tropical storm came up. Their ship was wrecked at the mouth of the Tana River. Though their lives were saved, the missionaries lost their outfits. Misfortune followed them up country, for they settled in a malarial zone. Weakened and sick, some of them left for America, and others went to India.

Farther south the first Africa party suffered heavy blows as their leader, Andrew Haugerud, died as well as Mrs. Gullander. Paul Gullander took his motherless child home, and Carl Poulsen joined another mission. This left four women to fend for themselves in Swaziland. "The Lord is still your Shepherd," Franson wrote Malla Moe, "and you shall not want."

❖   ❖   ❖

In China the pioneers faced continual persecution and danger. When Peter Holmen entered Sian, the capital of Shensi, a teeming city of a million inhabitants, the officials discovered he was there and served notice that he must be out of the city in twenty-four hours.

"Oh, I can leave at once, but wouldn't you like to have me sing a song before I go?" he asked.

They agreed, so he picked up his guitar and sang a song for them in Chinese. They were pleased, and he sang another and another. The air which had been tense and threatening cleared. This jolly troubadour didn't seem to be much of a foreign devil. They consulted among themselves, saying, "This missionary is not like the rest of these foreigners we have heard about. Let's allow him to stay."

A guitar had opened the doors of one of the great, untouched cities of China. When Franson heard how Peter

Holmen had charmed a mob with music, he rejoiced. Sian became the center for the Mission's work, but before many months passed, robust, young Holmen was struck down by typhoid fever and died.

"Abrahamson, Olson, and now Holmen!" Franson exclaimed. "What a price is being paid to win our Chinese brethren to Christ! But no price is greater than that the Saviour has already paid."

He puzzled over the loss of these keen young missionaries, so greatly needed where they fell, and finally declared, "I sometimes think God takes them so they can give their full time to prayer."

The finances of the SAM dropped in 1894 and again in 1895. Hard times were general everywhere, and the missionaries had not had large allowances to begin with. Not that the missionaries were complaining; it was others in the homelands who predicted worse things to come.

Franson moved through this confusion with the freshness and simplicity of a child, yet with the brisk, self-assurance of a general. "I shall go and see the situation on the mission fields for myself," he announced.

Then he preached a sermon which showed the secret of his overflowing confidences. It was based on Psalm 87:7, "All my springs are in thee":

> Not everybody can say, "All my springs are in God." There are thousands who have all their springs in the world. They love the pleasures and satisfactions of the world and want nothing to do with God.
>
> There are even believing souls who cannot say, "All my springs are in God." Only part of their springs are in Him, and the rest in other things. Some may love God, but they love their children so intensely and exclusively that if one of them dies they are comfortless.

Some find their whole satisfaction in the property they own, and if that is lost they lose confidence and hope. Such people, of course, do not have all their springs in God.

The spring of true joy is found in God. So is the spring of power. We all need much wisdom, and the spring for this is also found in Him. I once asked a little five-year-old boy whether he could write. He answered, "Yes, I can write everything if Daddy holds and guides my hand." We lack wisdom to serve unless God holds and guides our hand.

Then, too, the spring of endurance is in God. There are those who had their springs in God five or ten years ago, but they have left the precious Fountain of Life and can no longer say, "All my springs are in God." The question which is all-important is not whether your springs have been or hope to be in God, but just now—this day, this moment—can you truly say, "All my springs are in Thee"? Then you may rejoice in always being with the Lord. Jesus said, "The water that I shall give him shall be in him a well of water springing up into eternal life."

How fantastic it seemed from a worldly point of view! Here was a grown man talking about having childlike faith. With hardly a cent in his pockets, he calmly proposed a trip around the world.

God met him on the plane of faith on which he was walking. A wealthy but devoted Christian woman, Miss Katherine Juell, asked for the privilege of paying his travel expenses. He was delighted that the Mission should be relieved of such a burden and thanked her cordially.

With that he left Sweden on his way to India. There was no fanfare except for the faithful friends who insisted on being present at the Malmo dockside. As the ropes were cast off and the gap widened between ship and shore, they sang one hymn after another until he felt the lump in his throat would choke him. What multiplied brothers and sisters in the Lord he had! He knew they stood with him in the battle for souls.

Chapter 20

TIBETANS FOR CHRIST

TOM-TOM, RATTLE, RATTLE! Tom-tom, rattle, rattle! Franson awoke to the unaccustomed sound, slipped out of his bedroll, dressed, and walked out into the pale fog which swathed the town of Ghoom, India. He passed shuttered houses and the village well. A dog started to bark, and several others joined it in a growing frenzy of excitement. He passed the tent of some Tibetan pilgrims where an old woman was boiling the morning tea. She paid no attention to him, but kept up a steady chant of heathen prayer.

He had but recently arrived in India and, after the heat of the plains, welcomed the briskness of the mountain air. He walked along the Jalapahar ridge toward Darjeeling until he found a spot where he saw the clouds lifting and the tips of Kanchenjunga breaking through. He sat and prayed in a growing ecstasy as the sun began to tint the snow peaks pink. The massive face of Kanchenjunga came alive with light. It seemed suspended between the blue sky and the cotton cloud bank in the lower valleys. Franson broke out in the Swedish strains of "A Mighty Fortress Is Our God."

In prayers with the missionaries later that morning in "Evelyn Cottage," this was still in his mind. He said, "The snow mountains are here in front of us, stretching as

126

far as we can see from east to west. They are like the ramparts of an impenetrable fortress, blocking our way into Tibet. But God made even them, and they are His. As we pray for the opening of Tibet to the gospel, let us remember Luther's hymn 'A mighty fortress is our God, a bulwark never failing.'"

John Fredrickson and the other missionaries had been studying the language for two years and were just at the point where they wanted to spread out and occupy new stations along the frontier. They brought out their maps and showed the various possibilities to Franson.

"To the east of Bhutan is Sadiya," Shoberg explained, "and there the Bramaputra River flows down out of Tibet with waters, some of which have come from Lhasa itself. I'd like to go there."

"Our most promising lead is over the border in Bhutan," Fredrickson explained. "I got permission from the government in Punakha to build a station near Ghunabatti. It's a place called Baksa Duar, right on one of the trade routes down into India. The house is nearly finished now, and some of the ladies are hoping to move over there."

Gustafson joined in to say, "When we men were living in Darjeeling with the explorer Sarat Chandra Das, he kept urging us to go north from here into Sikkim. The largest caravans from Tibet come right down through Lachung and follow the Teesta River valley on to Kalimpong."

"And what about all this area to the west of Nepal?" Franson asked, running his finger along the border.

"We haven't been over there yet, but we're hoping that you'll get along with us to Mussoorie and the other points where we might locate Tibetans," Fredrickson said. "Will you have time?"

"I'll stay with you just as long as I'm needed," he declared.

Franson felt that the purpose of his trip was to encourage the missionaries and to spur them on. They themselves were still so very new to the work that they looked to him for advice. He commended them for the schools they had opened in four nearby villages. With seven single women on the field, this work for children seemed a very appropriate approach.

He escorted two of the ladies to the new station at Baksa Duar, and part of the way through the low-lying forests they rode on elephants. Because the region was noted for man-eating tigers, they offered special prayer for protection against wild animals. As they jogged along, however, Franson couldn't help calling out to his companions, "Wouldn't it be thrilling to see a tiger?"

Emma Swenson and Beda Elofson shuddered at the idea. "I don't think you are being very consistent, Mr. Franson," Miss Swenson objected. "After all, you prayed very earnestly to God to keep the tigers away!"

During the next months Franson tramped hundreds of miles over mountain trails with his fellow workers. He reached the border of Tibet at the Nilang Pass and looked with longing at the nomad tents and grazing herds on the plateau below him. "Oh, I'd love to go into the land myself," he said to Shoberg and Gustafson. "I know that the British district commissioners don't approve, and the Tibetan government is suspicious. But it would be worth a try. How would you like to be sewn up in a yak skin and go in as a piece of merchandise?"

"The skin would dry and shrink and crush you to death," Shoberg replied.

"Well—we could disguise ourselves as Tibetans and take our Gospels in as pack loads," Franson said, undaunted.

"You, Mr. Franson, with your blue eyes—do you think you could fool a Tibetan for a minute?"

"Oh, I guess you're right," he said. "But it is fun thinking about anyway."

He realized that converted Indians or Tibetans would be strategic messengers of the gospel to Tibet, and he used every opportunity to urge this task on national Christians. Failing this, he continued to witness daily to the unsaved.

One evening Franson reached a government rest house in Sikkim and stopped for the night. These places were built at regular stages along main routes. The caretakers provided rooms and cooking facilities for a modest sum, but you had to bring your own food.

A handsome young Eurasian was already there, and they would share quarters in the bungalow that night. His name was MacDonald but his Tibetan mother had firmly ingrained Buddhism in his mind and heart.

They started to talk, for MacDonald was fluent in English as well as Tibetan and Hindi. He regaled Franson with stories of his travel up and down the trails as an interpreter for government expeditions.

"I can think of an even better job for you," Franson said.

The young MacDonald pricked up his ears. "What's that, sir?" he asked.

"Giving your life to the King of kings and serving Him."

They launched into a long argument, for MacDonald was determined to defend Buddhism as superior to Chris-

tianity. "You are trying to convert me," he said, "so I'll
try and convert you."

Finally Franson said, "We are accomplishing nothing
by this. Come, get down on your knees before the living
God."

The suggestion enraged MacDonald, and he refused.
Franson went ahead and knelt down. As he prayed one of
his gripping, faith-filled prayers, conviction stole into the
young man's heart. By the time Franson was finished,
MacDonald was on the floor beside him, weeping. Franson led him to Christ. This man later was stationed as
British trade agent at Yatung in the Chumbi Valley of
Tibet. There he won others to Christ and organized the
first group of believers in the closed land.

Along this same route Franson came on a young Tibetan man lying by the wayside, sick and alone. He spoke
to him through an interpreter, and the fellow said hopelessly, "I'm dying! I'm dying!"

"If you are dying, you can go to heaven—if you believe
in Jesus Christ," Franson told him. There on the trail he
led him to the Lord. Then he arranged for him to be
taken to a hospital. The new convert rallied and lived for
two more years of joyful testimony.

As the missionaries scattered to the new stations and
settled into their work, Franson took time to write a
booklet on the errors of Buddhism, *The Religion of Tibet*.
He also wrote several tracts, all of which were translated
and printed on a mission press in Calcutta. "You could
use a Tibetan press up here in the hills," he told Fredrickson. "And when I get back to the States I hope the Lord
will give me one for you."

At the end of six months Franson decided his ministry
in India was completed, and he bade his friends, both

foreign and national, farewell. "We'll meet again in heaven, Tsering!" he said to the Tibetan he had rescued from death.

Chapter 21

STRENGTHENING THE BRETHREN

T HOUGH FRANSON STOPPED BRIEFLY in South China with some Scandinavian missionaries, he headed for Japan before making an intensive tour of China. The Scandinavian Alliance missionaries in Japan lived mostly in and around Tokyo, but they already had twelve stations and thirty outstations. In spite of financial stringency, they were supporting fourteen Japanese fellow workers out of their personal funds.

For his missionaries and Japanese evangelists Franson held a two-week course on evangelism which finished with a day of fasting and prayer on the anniversary of the arrival of the Japan party.

He felt that the missionaries needed to fan out into some of the other thickly populated areas of the country, and with this in mind he prospected for new fields.

He endeared himself to the Japanese workers by his consideration for them and his passion for souls. They were much impressed by the time he spent in meditation and prayer, a characteristic expected of a true holy man by Eastern ideals.

When some of the missionaries urged him to have one meeting in Swedish, especially for them, he objected on the basis that the Japanese brethren would not be able to understand. He did not want to exclude them. One of the young lady missionaries exclaimed impulsively, "Oh, if you do not preach to us in Swedish, we will return to America!"

"My fellow worker," he replied, "that is no way to talk, even in fun."

He did give in, however. And after his sermon in Swedish, the young lady said gratefully, "That was like honey on our bread, to hear a sermon in our own language."

"It is bread *and* honey to the Japanese when we can preach the gospel to them in *their* mother tongue," he replied.

He made a plea from Japan to home supporters to be faithful to their missionaries overseas in prayer and giving. He cited one of the workers who had received only ten dollars one quarter instead of the promised sixty dollars. "Such things ought not to be," he declared. "The Lord will call everyone to account who neglects to fulfill a promise given in His name for His work."

Moving on, Franson reached Shanghai on New Year's Eve. Hudson Taylor and the friends of the China Inland Mission were as usual spending the day in prayer for the year ahead. He gladly joined them. This was his first opportunity to meet Taylor face to face, though he had prayed for him for almost fifteen years. "I feel that I met you through George Müller," he said, "for on our trip together across the Atlantic he told me so much about you."

Speaking later to a meeting of CIM missionaries he said, "I am very much at home among you because so many of the young people I have sent out here are in your fellowship. And as I look around me here, I cannot help but think of the fifty from America who received the hospitality of this compound four years ago. Altogether there are over one hundred and fifty missionaries in this great land for whom I feel some responsibility. It has been good for them that so many of them have been associated with you. This has helped them to combine Scandinavian modesty with American dash and British perseverance, a combination which should make them good missionaries."

Franson then embarked on a seven-month tour of the provinces of the interior, encouraging the young missionaries and entering into their labors. At Changsha he rejoiced when for the first time he witnessed a Chinese cry out and confess his sins under his preaching. "I was beginning to think that these people were as stolid as the Danes," he said. "But now I see how the fire of the Holy Spirit melts them too."

Coming to the station of D. E. Hoste and his wife, Franson held special meetings in the church. A great spirit of prayer gripped the Christians, and this prepared the way for a public meeting in which more than half of the audience came forward to the front to make decisions. In his closing prayer Franson said, "Lord, help us to believe until we really believe!" He wanted genuine conviction, sincere repentance, and clear-cut decisions for Christ. This had been the pattern in his own life which had kept him on a steady course.

Reaching Shensi, Franson crossed the Sian plain and entered the great gates of the city which Peter Holmen had opened with a guitar. The mission chapel and compound lay on the busy main street of Sian. One of his first privileges was to baptize the first three converts of the Scandinavian Alliance Mission there. "Thank you, dear God, for these three," he prayed. "But, O Lord, why not three thousand souls?"

The Lord heard this prayer and gave far more than three thousand in the years that followed as missionaries of the SAM (later called TEAM) took up the challenge.

Scanning a large map, he began to confer with the missionaries as to how best they could spread out and fill the whole province of Shensi with a witness for Christ. He told them what had been done in India and Japan. He described the work he had seen downcountry in China —Sunday schools, day schools, opium-recovery clinics, dispensaries, and outstations.

"What a joy it was for me to see the fruit of Emanuel Olson's ministry down in Kwei-hua-cheng and Pao-tou," he said. "When I held meetings in those stations we saw more souls come to the Lord. The non-Christians all knew and respected Olson, and I found no better appeal to make to get the people to accept Christ and to live wholly for Him, than to ask them whether they didn't want to meet Nga mu-shih (Olson's Chinese name) in heaven. We visited his grave, and when I looked at the mound where his body lay, I could not restrain my tears. I felt I could somewhat understand the feelings of Jesus when he stood at the grave of Lazarus and groaned in spirit. Praise God! Death shall be overcome. Come soon, Lord Jesus!"

Pin-chou, Chenchiakou, Lantien, Yingchiawei, Pingliang, Chingchou, Sifengchen, and Changwu—eight main stations were opened that year of 1895 as the missionaries responded to Franson's fiery messages.

"You need a press here even more than the missionaries in India," he said. "You have no printing facilities nearby. I certainly am going to make this a matter of prayer. Think what it would mean if you could print your own tracts and hymnbooks and perhaps a magazine."

His mind raced ahead. He could see so much to do in China, and he would not have been willing to leave for North America if he had not felt that he could thereby better serve the cause of Christ.

Chapter 22

FREDRIK FRANSON,
GENERAL DIRECTOR

Come, sit upon my knee, Nora," Franson invited his seven-year-old niece. He was back in Nebraska, visiting his brothers' and sisters' families. They were enthralled by his tales of faraway lands.

"Tell me for whom you are named," he said.

"For your old hometown in Sweden," she said proudly.

"That's right. Now do you know what your name spells backward?"

"A–r–o–n. It spells 'Aron,' doesn't it?"

"Yes, and who was Aaron?"

"I know," she said with delight. "He was Moses' brother!"

"Oh, good for you!" he declared, his face wreathed in smiles. "Of course, Aaron has an extra *a* at the front, but you can always remember that your name has a connection with him. He was a spokesman for Moses. I hope you will be a person who speaks for the Lord Jesus Christ."

He began probing to find out how much she understood about the gospel, then placing his hand on her head, prayed for her.

As she slid from his lap and ran out the door, he turned to her mother and said, "This child is not far from the kingdom."

He did not hesitate during his brief visits home to deal with all his relatives, large and small, and he claimed them all for the Lord. Of those who held back he said confidently, "They will be saved," and he was not mistaken. Each one for whom he prayed eventually made a clear commitment to Christ.

"Uncle Fredrik, how do you speak to strangers about Jesus?" one of the younger generation asked.

"Well, some of your best opportunities are when you make a trip, for instance, if you were going in to Omaha. When you see an empty seat in a railway car, if there's one person there, always take that seat beside a person. If you're a man, find a place with a man. If you're a woman, find a place with a woman.

"Then, after you have remarked about this and that, you can say something like this: 'Isn't the Lord God good to us?'

"If it is raining, you can say, 'Think how kind the Lord is that He gives us rain so things won't dry up.'

"If the sun shines, say, 'Isn't God good to give sunshine?'

"They'll usually agree with you, and then you say, 'Do you know God?' And before you know it, you can contact the person; and when you get him to say, 'Yes, I really should be a Christian,' you reply, 'Well, this is a good time.' Now just lean toward him, and, if you have a hat, you can hold it before your face. This way you can pray quietly with the person, and you don't need to cause any attention from others on the train. You can lead souls to the Lord that way."

Franson could not stay long in Nebraska because the

board of the Scandinavian Alliance Mission was waiting
for him in Chicago, eager to hear his report from the fields.
When he arrived at the mission office, he found Risberg
finishing an interview with a missionary candidate. "Go
right on," he said. "Don't let me interrupt."

He seated himself on a high bookkeeper stool and
watched Risberg in his swivel chair and the nervous young
man standing beside him.

"You're from the farm, aren't you?" Risberg asked.

"Yes," the candidate replied.

"Well, I don't suppose you need any physical examination then," Risberg said. "We will be glad to let you go
this fall if you have your support."

They joined together in a time of prayer, and the young
man left.

"I'm glad to see another young missionary in the
making," Franson said.

"Yes, and I'm glad to see you, dear brother," Risberg
replied. "We need you to answer some of the questions
which have piled up."

"Yes, I know," Franson sighed. "The work of a mission
director in the home country seems to be largely taken
up with answering people's questions."

"We are hoping you will take the post of general director when we have the annual meeting this winter," Risberg went on. "We have been working on the constitution,
and we have made provision for you as that leader."

"But I am on the move so much. Isn't there one of you
who live here who would take this position?"

"None of us can give the leadership you can as the
founder and as the one who has visited the fields. You
have no idea how well your letters from various countries
have been received."

Franson accepted his duties as general director in 1896, then immediately began to plan missionary meetings all over the States. As he moved from church to church, one of the problems which caught his attention was the need for more cooperation among the free churches. The SAM missionaries came from different denominations, but they were almost identical in doctrine and church order. These missionaries worked in happy fellowship on the fields. He wondered why the same couldn't be true in the homeland. As he mentioned this thought to others he found that they accepted it in theory. No one, however, was prepared to crusade for this closer association.

Although he failed to unite these church groups, in the Midwest he succeeded in forming some ministerial fellowships that brought Christian workers from different but like-minded denominations together.

Sometimes he was asked to advise regarding odd problems. During a tour of the eastern states, he visited a church in Danbury, Connecticut. At the close of a Saturday evening meeting, the pastor drew Franson to one side and said, "I have a married couple here who wish to talk with you. They came to me last week, but knowing you were coming, I asked them to wait and discuss their difficulties with you."

When the couple came to speak with him, he discovered they wanted his sanction for them to divorce one another.

"Divorce!" he burst out. "You want to separate? No, get down on your knees and ask God to save you!"

The result was that they got right with the Lord and were also reconciled to one another.

When Franson and the pastor returned to the manse

to relax over cups of hot cocoa, the visiting evangelist turned the conversation to the history of New England.

"If I remember rightly it was here in Danbury where David Brainerd was licensed to preach the gospel," he said.

"Oh, is that so? I never realized that before," the pastor replied.

"Yes, this countryside used to be a base for missions to the Indians, and Brainerd was one of the first to go. What a man of prayer he was!"

Then he proceeded to unfold some of his own experiences in prayer in an effort to help his brother pastor.

Upon returning to Chicago, he happened to drop in at Salem Church at a time when the pastor and one of the church officers were having a discussion which turned into an argument. They disagreed over which one should have authority in a certain matter. As their voices rose, Franson prayed at one side. He sobbed. Tears flowed down his cheeks. He got up and walked back and forth. At last he came over to the two men. Placing his left hand on the pastor's shoulder and his right hand on the other man's shoulder, he looked at them. They stared at him in silence.

Then he said, "Brethren, be very careful about hard words. They wound so easily, and they are so hard to heal."

Chapter 23

PERSISTENT SOUL-WINNER

W ISHING TO GET OUT and away from city areas for a while Franson accepted revival services in the northern part of Minnesota. There he visited every home in the community, even the humblest log cabins. Where folk would not come out to hear him, he went and preached the gospel directly to them. The local schoolhouse was packed out as Franson gave his threefold message: "Come to Jesus; go for Jesus; wait for Jesus." He wanted souls to be saved, and he wanted every saved soul to be doing something in service for Christ. Furthermore, he wanted every believer to love the thought of Christ's return. "We cannot all be good-looking," he jested, "but we can all be good lookers!"

He had been preaching the second coming of Christ for twenty years, and the subject was as fresh to him as it ever had been. He felt it was eminently practical, for he had seen it bring sinners to the foot of the cross and take saints to the ends of the earth.

Even when resting in Colorado Springs this was uppermost in his mind. For instance, he had been praying for two hours early one morning and then had gone back to bed. It was a cloudy morning, but the sun suddenly broke through the clouds. The rays of bright sunlight fell full in the face of the sleeping man. It awakened him, and he jumped up in a daze, crying, "Lord Jesus, have you come at last?"

What a disappointment when he discovered the Lord had not come yet! "Ah, well, it will be soon," he said.

When his companion, Gustaf F. Johnson, suggested one day that they join a party of fishermen, he borrowed a pole and went along. After a bit his pole bent down, and he pulled in a dogfish. "Oh, see what a good fish I caught!" he exclaimed.

One of the other fishermen said, "No, that's no good at all. You can't eat that. You don't eat dogfish."

"Is that so?" he replied. "Well, help me take it off the hook, and I'll try again."

Before long the cork went down again, and when he pulled up his line, he had a dangling turtle.

This time he really was disgusted. "Now I believe I've got an old sea hag," he said. "That's enough fishing for me. I'll go downstream and have a swim."

He was an excellent swimmer, but one of the men warned him, "Don't forget, the water's cold!"

"I've been in some streams in the Himalayan Mountains so cold I don't think you'd dare take a bath in them," he declared. "I like it cold. Up on some of those high Tibetan passes, I would take my shoes and socks off and tramp around for a few minutes in the snow. It sure was good for sore feet! Anybody want to come with me?"

"Not for us!" his companions said, and off he went alone for his dip.

* * *

Franson heard that John Lundeen, a student from Chicago Theological Seminary, was preaching in the Community Church at Idaho Springs, so he went down with

Johnson to see him. The three of them were standing talking by a mineral water spring when they saw a young lady approaching.

"Now, Lundeen," Franson said, "we've got to try to win this young lady for the Lord. We may never see her again. Do you know her?"

"No, I don't know her. She's a stranger here," he said.

"Well, this is our one chance. We may never see her again."

With that he took a tin cup and washed it out. Then full to the brim, he offered it to her as she came by. She said, "Thank you," and accepted it.

When she drank that, Franson said, "May I offer you another cup?"

"Thank you," she said.

While she was drinking again, he said, "Young lady, do you know anything about the living water?"

"Oh," she said, "you mean about religion?"

"Well, not exactly that," he said. "There's a good deal of religion with no living water in it. You know, living water is more than religion."

With that he proceeded to explain the gospel to her, and she showed her interest.

"What do you say, young lady? Shall we bow our heads? We'll probably never meet again in this world. Shouldn't we appoint a meeting above the stars of heaven?"

She said, "Yes, sir, we ought to."

"If you'll bow your head, we'll do that," he said.

He prayed a fervent prayer, and at the end the young woman thanked him, her eyes wet with tears.

That was the last time he saw her, but he felt sure she had accepted Christ. That night he held a meeting in the church, and it was crowded with miners and townsfolk.

He talked over his strategy with Johnson and Lundeen. "I'm going to speak first on my travels in Palestine. Then I'm going to give them a missionary address. Then I'll speak on the coming of the Lord and, last of all, revival. After the meeting, Johnson, I want you to meet with the Christians and get them to subscribe to missions. Lundeen, you go to the door and stand there so people can't get out, and I'll deal with the unsaved."

It is amazing, but he completed his entire message in half an hour. There were only seven Christians present, and Johnson began talking to them up at the front while Franson went from bench to bench in the aftermeeting.

He asked one young man, "Are you a Christian?"

He answered, "No."

"Don't you want to be one?"

"Oh, well—why not?" the fellow replied.

"All right, get down on your knees!"

That scared the young man, and he tried to get away from Franson, who had a tight grip on him. They began to swing around in a circle, and this broke up the meeting.

As the others rushed out the door Lundeen cried, "Wait, friends, wait—no hurry." But they pushed him over and ran on out.

The young man, finally free of Franson, picked himself up, raced out, and knocked Lundeen down again. Franson stood in the middle of the floor with folded hands, praying. "O Lord," he said, "who took the people away? Did the devil take them all?"

The next morning they were invited to a miner's home for breakfast. While they were sitting there eating, they were startled to see this same young man come in. This was his home. He started to eat breakfast with them, but when Franson tackled him again on spiritual matters, he got up and ran out. Franson was after him, chasing him for several blocks, but the young fellow got away.

When Franson came back, he turned to the boy's mother and said, "What do you say? Shall we ask God to catch him? I couldn't."

The mother broke down. "Yes," she sobbed.

"Well, if he runs too hard, God might break a leg so he can't run," he warned.

"It's better to have a broken leg than to have both hands and feet and be lost," she said.

"Do you really believe that, sister?" he asked.

"Yes," she said.

"Then, let's pray."

Down they knelt. Then in all solemnity he prayed, "Lord, if the young man runs too fast, break a leg. And if he doesn't stop, Lord, break the other one too."

As they were praying, the young man came back in and knelt between his mother and Franson. The tears rolled down his cheeks until there were patches on the carpetless floor.

Franson rejoiced in the son's repentance. "I thought God would get you," he told him. "You did well not to run too fast!"

* * *

Near the end of two years of such itinerating in the States, Franson began to plan another trip to Europe. He talked this over with Professor Nyvall at North Park College. "This will be my third time back to Sweden, and I continue to get letters from there inviting me over to speak on prophetic subjects. This has always greatly moved hearts there."

He got hold of paper and pencil and began to make some calculations about prophetic timing, but Nyvall was not interested. "My dear Brother Franson," he said, "can't you come to some conclusion without so much addition and subtraction?"

Franson smiled and pushed the paper to one side. "I know what you're thinking," he said. "You feel that this is a waste of time. Moody does too. He says he knows of nothing that moves the church away from the world more than telling people to wait for Christ's coming. In my experience, however, I have found that preaching on the Lord's soon return bolsters missionary concern and gets the Christians to witnessing."

"Just be careful," Nyvall replied, still somewhat unconvinced.

"Brother Nyvall, did you know Martin Luther looked for the Lord's return, but he was very practical about it? He once said, 'If I knew today that Jesus was coming tomorrow, I would still plant a tree.' For myself I am working as well as waiting. I want a good home base for the missions. That has been my aim here in the States and that will be my aim over in the old country."

That summer of 1898 he was back in Sweden.

Chapter 24

CONSTANT CLOSE COMMUNION

FRANSON HAD BEEN WELCOMED into the home of the famous Swedish evangelist, Karl Anderson, and the two men talked late into the night. Even after they had crawled into their beds, they kept up their discussion. Suddenly Franson leaped from his bed and began to sing a chorus:

> "Then lift I white wings, white wings,
> And hurry my way home."

Karl Anderson remained hunched up under his bedcovers. His temperament was entirely different from this exuberant Swedish-American.

Finally he said, "Yes, Franson, you sing and rejoice in the coming glory. Do you know how it seems to me? I lie awake at night and cry and pray for the miserable human beings who will not believe the gospel. Yes, when in my vision I see all of Sweden's Satan-bound prisoners like a long, clinking chain passing by me, I shed bitter tears. I am debtor to all. I am under bonds to give them the gospel."

"My heart cries out for them too," Franson replied. "I feel a debtor not only to Sweden but to the whole world. There is no tribe or nation where I would not like to go and preach the gospel. I could not go on if I did not remind myself of the power of the gospel and the assurance we have of victory. Do you know what I have written in the flyleaf of my Bible? It is what an old soldier engraved on his sword: 'Where I do not find a way I shall cut one!'"

"How different we two are," Anderson said, "and yet the Lord sees fit to use us both in His kingdom."

With all of his difference Franson was now received gladly in Scandinavia as a thoroughly seasoned evangelist and missionary who had proved himself. For three busy years he moved through Sweden, Norway, Germany, and Finland with more calls than he could fill.

In earlier years he had led the crown prince of Sweden, Oscar Bernadotte, to Jesus Christ. Prince Oscar had renounced his rights to the throne in order to give his life to Christian service. Now the prince opened many a door for Franson and sometimes traveled with him.

Christian workers who formerly had looked askance at Franson's ruthless dealing with unbelievers began to realize that he was a deft and even discreet surgeon of souls. They marveled at his zeal and good spirits. Then they watched him as the terrible tidings of the Boxer Uprising in China brought news of martyr deaths among missionaries and Chinese Christians.

How did Franson react under the strain of those summer days of 1900? As founder of six mission societies in Europe and one in America, he had an immediate job to do, comforting bereaved parents and encouraging disconsolate friends. He wrote to the families of five young missionaries murdered in Mongolia, the newest field of the Scandinavian Alliance Mission. Where it would seem words would have failed, his poured out in a healing stream.

The source of his power lay in prayer. He spent so much time on his knees that his trousers had to be repeatedly patched. He was a living example of what he preached—

constant, close communion with God. This tragedy that had struck him personally was only bearable because he could talk it over with his living Lord.

Gradually the news from China took a turn for the better. The devastation of Christian work had been great, but the tales of heroism and God's protection to many showed that the devil had overstepped himself. Franson called for new volunteers to take the place of those who had fallen.

At this time God laid on his heart those nations of Europe which he had not as yet visited. Since he liked to pray with maps spread out before him, he kept the world and all its peoples before him. Soon he was touring Holland, Belgium, France, Spain, Portugal, then Algeria, Greece, and Russia. He would have liked to go across Siberia to the Far East but decided that God wanted him to return first to the United States.

In the spring of 1902 the board of the Scandinavian Alliance Mission voted to make him General Director for life. He did not want this position and begged them to find someone living in Chicago to take the leadership of the mission. They would not accept his objections. "We'll find men to carry on the office work," they said. "Why, you do more for the welfare of the mission by your missionary tours than you would here!"

Then, to his surprise and embarrassment, they prepared a special festival in his honor. He was presented with a beautiful new Bible and other gifts.

"I don't know why I should be receiving these presents," he said. "I guess we should consider this my fiftieth birthday celebration, for it is coming along soon."

After the great day and all the kind speeches were over, Franson took the new Bible and left it with a friend in Chicago. "I'll come for it the next time I come back to this country," he explained, "but I want to keep my old one for the present. I've written so much in it, and it is underlined. I'm not ready to use a new one."

Visiting Duluth, Minnesota, he had this worn, old Bible with him as he conducted children's meetings. One Sunday morning he spoke in a Sunday School, and several boys and girls went forward for salvation, among them young Paul Rood. Rood was only six years old, but he was soundly converted. Later he would be a prime mover in getting the Child Evangelism movement under way in the United States.

In Dawson, Minnesota, when Franson was called to a home where a mother lay dying, he quickly sized up the situation—the distraught husband, the restless children. "Let us pray," he said quietly. "Oh God," he prayed, "You see this dear woman and her large family. The children are still small, and they need her to bring them up to know Thee. Spare her, Lord, for the sake of these small ones in this home, in Jesus' name. Amen."

The mother rallied immediately, and God permitted her to live many more years with her family.

What an amazingly adaptable man he was! Moving from country to country, from Christians to non-Christians, from home to home, he seemed equally at ease in each situation. He did not dominate others; he let the Holy Spirit dominate. He did not push himself forward; rather he introduced his constant companion, Jesus Christ.

Visiting for a meal in the home of a large clan of Olsons, Franson realized that some of the family were not Christians. Just as they all sat down to eat, he said, "Let us pray." While he prayed, conviction of sin fell on the un-

saved members of the family, and they themselves began
to plead with God for salvation.

Here was a man to whom prayer was as breathing. He
could lead others into a spirit of prayer. Once, while he
was staying with the parents of a missionary, he interrupted the early morning bustle of the wife, saying, "Mrs. Nelson, couldn't you leave the breakfast dishes as they are,
and couldn't we have a season of prayer right now?"

"Yes," said the godly woman, "we'll leave them."

Then he prayed with the Nelsons and his traveling companion, Gustaf Johnson, throughout the morning and on
into the afternoon. They kept on until five o'clock. By that
time Franson had somehow tangled his feet in some
drapes and couldn't get loose. "Johnson," he said, "we'll
have to stop praying. Come and help me get free."

Prayer was his recourse when a pastor in Nebraska at-
tacked him bitterly at the end of a meeting. "You had no
right to appeal for missionary contributions without con-
sulting our church board first and getting their permission," he said.

Franson accepted this public dressing down quietly,
apologized, and walked from the platform. That evening
he said to his companion, "Ask the people here if there
isn't another room where you can sleep because I want to
be alone tonight."

It was arranged, and Franson was by himself. The
reason he wanted privacy was that he might spend the
whole night in prayer for the pastor.

* * *

It was in quiet times of personal devotion that Franson
formulated his plans for another pilgrimage to faraway
mission fields. He decided to go to the Far East by a cir-
cuitous route that would take him into the southern hemis-

phere. Frank Gustafson, a young missionary, was to accompany him.

They sailed from San Francisco in August, 1902, stopping in Honolulu, and then heading southward through
calm waters. One day Franson was sitting on deck, reading his Greek New Testament, when Gustafson came running to tell him that they were crossing the equator. At
that point Franson was reading John 2:5, "Whatsoever
he saith unto you, do it."

He looked out at the blue Pacific. They were entering
the South Seas. Then he lifted his heart to the Lord.
"What is it You want me to do?" he mused. The thought
came to him that he should pray for New Zealand, Australia, the South Sea Islands, which lay before him. He also
prayed for gospel witnesses in Borneo, Java, South Africa,
and South America. He believed prayer was one of his
major responsibilities in God's service, and he took it seriously.

* * *

After some months, Franson left Australia behind, sailed
up to Canton, moved slowly through the coastal provinces
of China, then crossed to Japan.

As he saw Japanese congregations once again, leaving
their shoes at the doors and sitting back on their heels
on the straw matting, he confided to the missionaries, "I
like to preach to people like this who are down on their
knees. They are already well on the way to being saved!"

The SAM work had developed in the four districts of
Tokyo, Chiba, Izu, and Hida. There Franson plunged into
city meetings and country evangelism. As he traveled
around with missionary Joel Anderson, he said, "I wish I
could speak Japanese the way you do, for you can deal

personally with the people concerning God and in their own language."

He did what he could. Entering a village, he would lead the evangelistic team. He couldn't sing with them as they marched along, but he would lift his arm and point skyward to indicate that these were envoys from the God of heaven.

The team wearied before he did. Even when they all withdrew to the mountains for a rest Franson was keen for long walks and spirited calisthenics. Although Joel Anderson was a young man with less than three years on the mission field, he was no match for this veteran with his sprinkling of gray hair among the black. Franson often winded Anderson in physical exercise, and he spent more time in prayer and Bible study. Years later the lingering impression he left with the Japanese pastors was this diligence in his daily devotions.

On the day the group was to leave their mountain retreat a violent rainstorm blew up. In prayers that morning Franson asked God to shut the windows of heaven, but the downpour continued. One young missionary became increasingly restless over the delay and finally insisted that they start out in the rain. Franson wanted to wait for his prayer to be answered, but he gave in to the wishes of the majority. Down the mountain trail they slipped and slithered, paper umbrellas blown to shreds, and clothes drenched. Franson held to his faith and partway down he called out, "Now, friends, we are going to give thanks to God who has heard our prayers." He led them in prayer, and they continued on their way.

Not much later the clouds broke, and the sun came out. Franson, who led the way as usual, stopped and waited for a lady missionary to catch up with him. "Do you remember, sister, what I said to you?" he asked.

Then without waiting for an answer, he turned and continued down the path. Anderson caught up with the lady just then, and he asked her what Franson had meant. She looked ruefully at her watch and said, "When we were leaving the inn, Mr. Franson told me that if we would wait until 11 o'clock the rain would stop. I was provoked with him and said, 'Who knows when this storm will be over? As long as we must go anyway, let us start at once.' I had my way, but do you see what time it is? It is just eleven."

Franson said no more about the matter. He knew the lesson had gone home.

His thoughts now turned to Korea and China. He had been invited by Dr. R. A. Hardie, of Wonsan, to come there for meetings, and in October, 1903, he answered this call. God so mightily used Franson in the Korean church that Dr. Hardie felt he was the forerunner who prepared the way for the great revivals of 1907 and 1908. Thanking his fellow missionary, Mr. Burkwall, who had recommended Franson to him, he said, "He was the man God used to teach us how to pray for revival and how to pray in a revival."

Franson's close fellowship with his Lord and Saviour brought him close fellowship with God's people everywhere. He was a mission leader touring the SAM fields, but he could not limit his prayers and his interests to the Scandinavian Alliance Mission. After all, the Holy Spirit led him to both his own missionaries and to a wider ministry as well.

Chapter 25

IF TWO WIN ONE

THE RAYS OF THE WESTERING SUN crept slowly across the earthen floor of the Chinese storefront. They were already over the wooden sill which cupped the door planks at night. They probed under the rough, wooden benches and then began to pick out details in a motley audience that was listening to two foreign preachers.

A gospel meeting was in process. The sunlight revealed Mongols in their sheepskins and leather boots as well as Chinese in padded winter cottons. This was Saratsi on the northern borders of China. Except for two shaven lamas, the rest all had queues of braided hair, for the Manchu Dowager Empress still held sway, tottering though her reign was. The sun glinted when it touched the sleek, black hair of the Chinese, but the Mongols' braids were tangled and dusty.

Franson was preaching to this come-and-go congregation with the help of Emil Jacobson, an old friend of the Berlin campaigns. They had been reunited in this border town when Franson came inland by slow stages, stopping for meetings all along the way. This was the last mission station, the end of the line. When he headed westward, Franson would not see another Christian chapel for hundreds of miles.

The preacher and his interpreter were often interrupted. Once a hen started to cluck and struggle to get loose in the robe of a nomad. The man got up abruptly, and several companions followed him. Others soon took their place, for the chapel was on a busy street.

Franson knew how to cope with restive crowds. He fascinated them with stories, first of all from their own country in which he had traveled more widely than they. He had been in the western provinces. A year before he had traveled from Canton in the South up the coast to Shanghai. Recently he had been in Shantung and Manchuria, hearing stories of bravery and faithful witness during the Boxer persecutions of 1900.

His eyes roved steadily from face to face, sizing up their reactions and looking for signs of spiritual hunger. He was pleased to be teamed with another missionary who was in complete harmony with him. Both men were equally minded to persuade men to believe in Jesus Christ.

Franson brought his hearers around to their own locale. "You will remember what happened three and a half years ago," he said. "Five of our missionary friends were murdered not far from here. Some Christians were killed in this very city. They were not afraid to die because they knew their sins were forgiven. They knew the way to God. My friends, I come from a far country. I have traveled many miles to tell you the good news that you can find the way to God too."

He told them of Jesus and His death, and how He rose alive again. The setting sun shone full in the face of both speakers. Franson pointed out the doorway and exclaimed, "The sun is going down, and soon it will be night! Your life is no more than a day, and then it is past. Are you ready to die?"

When the two men made an appeal, one young fellow came forward. Others might have come, but the two lamas stood up and strode out, laughing. This signaled a general break for the outside. Franson left Jacobson talking to the young inquirer and tried to restrain some from leaving. He even laid a firm hold on the sheepskin robe of a nomad, but the man shook his head and went out.

Franson returned to Jacobson and prayed beside him as he dealt with the one who had responded. He was a minor government clerk named Wang, and he made his decision to believe in Christ that day. Then, promising to come again for instruction, he bowed deeply and left.

The two missionaries were overjoyed. Together they began lifting the door planks into place for the night, leaving several of them out as a small entrance to the gospel hall. Their living quarters and that of the other missionaries on the station lay at the rear.

"Let's go for a walk before dark," Franson suggested to his fellow worker. They threaded their way through the streets to the city gate. Droves of sheep, goats, and cattle were being herded back into the city before nightfall. They watched the evening bustle for a few moments and then mounted the worn stone steps of the gate tower. At the top Franson looked around and said, "This reminds me of nine years ago when I first saw the Great Wall north of Peking. Our party of missionaries had a prayer meeting in one of the towers and asked God to break down the barricades in the hearts of these people."

"He certainly removed some prejudices in the heart of the man who just came to the Lord," Jacobson replied. "Wang told me he had been opposed to Christianity because it was a foreign religion. He said today as you spoke about the Chinese who were willing to die for

Christ, he realized it must be more than a foreign religion."

"Thank you, dear God," Franson murmured. Then, looking at Jacobson, he added, "As we were preaching together today I kept thinking of those days in Berlin. There we were, both speaking broken German, and they called us crazy Swedes. The ground used to seem hard at first, and then the Holy Spirit would begin to break up the pride and indifference."

"We had better music then than we had today," Jacobson said. "My one guitar and the autoharp are nothing like the choir we had there."

"Some of the people who came forward in those meetings are out on the mission fields today."

"Some others also, Pastor Franson," his companion said. "You are responsible for my sister and me being in China."

Franson looked at him with a smile. "Are you sorry, Jacobson?"

"No, of course not. These have been the happiest years of my life. It was back there in Germany in the mission hall you said, 'Follow me to China.' It was just like the Lord speaking through you to my heart."

"I believe it *was* the Lord who led you, not man," Franson said quietly.

It was almost dark as they descended to the street again. It was no longer crowded, and doors were beginning to slam shut for the night. At the gospel hall they barred the entrance and went back to the living quarters. The cozy dining room was lit by a large oil lamp in the middle of a round table. Jacobson's sister, Mrs. Oberg, and her husband and Mrs. N. J. Friedstrom were there. Friedstrom, who was the sole survivor of the pioneer missionaries to the Mongols, was away negotiating the rental of land at Patsebolong.

Mrs. Oberg apologized for the supper. "I'm afraid you will find the meat tough, Pastor Franson," she said. "At this altitude even hours of cooking don't make it tender."

"We'll thank the Lord then for good teeth," he remarked.

The conversation at the supper table continued long after the plates were empty and the teapot drained. The missionaries were eager to hear news of friends in the homelands and on other fields, and Franson was an inexhaustible mine of information. He told them of revivals, of answers to prayer, and of provisions of the Lord's mercy. He encouraged them with the word of new missionary candidates and movings of the Spirit on other stations. When the evening drew to an end, they sang a hymn and prayed together, encompassing the world in their prayers and not forgetting the new convert, Wang, who had just that day put his trust in Christ.

A week later Friedstrom arrived with the news that the Mongol chiefs had signed a land lease contract along with permission for the construction of an irrigation canal. "The papers I had from the American consul impressed them tremendously," he said.

Franson was delighted. "When we talked with the chiefs, I really was discouraged. They seemed so unreasonable in their demands," he said.

Friedstrom, a big hulk of a man, rubbed his hands together. "Now I can go ahead, but it will be a lot of work. It is going to take four hundred men to dig that canal from the Yellow River to our property. When the water comes in, we're going to see the desert blossom. That'll make the Mongols gather round!"

The talk turned to the coming of new missionaries, the Magnusens, and how Friedstrom would have to go east to Peking and escort them in. "I hope to bring in some seedlings when I come back," he said.

It was mid-January, and Franson was also planning to leave for the West and his visit to the Shensi field. Before either of them could get away, an emergency arose. One day after a meeting Jacobson looked hot and flushed. "I don't feel well," he said.

The fever rose, and on the fifth day when his sister saw the telltale spots of typhus, she went to her room and cried. Coming out again, she was composed, and a strange peace settled on the household.

In that remote place, far from hospital facilities or a doctor, there was little they could do. They took turns nursing the patient. In the second week he was often delirious.

One day Franson and Friedstrom were talking together. "It's almost impossible for us to protect ourselves against typhus," the younger man explained, "especially in the winter when the folk bundle themselves up and then huddle on the heated k'angs for warmth. If we kept to ourselves and did not visit in the homes, we would be safer, but we wouldn't be missionaries."

Jacobson grew weaker. Near the end Mrs. Oberg sat by her brother. "Emil," she called, "Emil!" His eyes opened. "Dear brother," she said, "take with you a loving greeting from us to the Saviour—and to all the dear ones who have gone to be with Him."

He understood, and he nodded slightly. Later when Franson came close, he whispered, "Jesus has ascended to heaven and has the keys. If two win one, then they win two."

These were his last words, and shortly the small group of missionaries was preparing for his funeral. Though they were numb with loss, they encouraged one another.

"Another gap in the ranks," Friedstrom said, "but God will fill it. I remember David Stenberg writing to me from here when I was still in the States preparing to come. He told me he was praying for a chain of hallelujah soldiers in central Asia that would stretch from sea to sea. David is gone, and now Emil, but God will still answer that prayer."

"Yes, I believe it," Franson told him, "and I wish that I could be one of them. Oh, do you know how I feel when I see someone I have called out here lay down his life? It tears my heart. I am responsible for so many who have come out to the mission field. And I knew what it would cost. John R. Mott of the Student Volunteer Movement says that one quarter of those who volunteer will lose their lives. How well I know it!"

The next day the large wooden coffin was carried laboriously out to a hillside behind the city. The missionaries and other local believers followed the eight straining coolies. Some curious spectators joined the train.

At the graveside the Christians sang hymns of triumph. No shrieks of anguish, no firecrackers, no discordant flutes and cymbals, as in most heathen funerals.

Then Franson spoke, using Oberg as his translator: "Our brother is not here, even though his body will lie beside that of other martyrs. Yes, he is a martyr too. Surely one who wears his body out in service for his Master is as much a martyr as the one whose head falls before the ax of his persecutors.

"He, like them, is in Paradise, free from all sufferings, and probably praying more earnestly than he could ever

IF TWO WIN ONE

do on earth for the spread of the good news of Jesus in this land."

Among those who had gathered round to listen was the new convert, Wang. Franson saw that he was standing with a group of men he did not recognize. Had Wang brought some non-Christian friends with him to the funeral? Afterward, Franson puzzled about this as he had puzzled about Jacobson's last statement. He became convinced that he had meant that if the two of them had won one soul, *that* one would win others. That is what he himself always prayed for each new convert on his prayer list.

The day after the funeral Franson had to leave Saratsi if he were to reach Shensi in time for the Scandinavian Alliance Mission conference. The mule litters were brought to the door of the gospel hall, one for Oberg who would accompany him to Sohpingfu, and one for himself. Two mules to a litter, one before and one behind, this mode of travel was not too uncomfortable, but the days of travel would be long. Oberg was far from well, but he was determined to escort Franson. The farewell prayers were full of faith in God's protection.

By the end of the first day, however, it was evident that Oberg was seriously ill. He had to be carried into the small Chinese inn. There Franson spent much of the night in prayer for his recovery, and in the morning Oberg felt much better.

"You must go back to Saratsi," Franson told him. "I will go on alone."

"How can you, Pastor Franson?" Oberg demurred. "You don't know how to speak Chinese. You will be helpless if any problem comes up."

"Nevertheless, you are not fit to go on. No, you must

go back. And I will not be alone, for God goes with me. Don't worry. We seem to have hired a good group of muleteers, and they will take me on."

Reluctantly Oberg consented to this change of plans. As they separated, Franson shook hands with him and said, "When we meet again, it will be with resurrection hands!"

Oberg tightened his grip and said, "Amen!" He shook his head and added, "I hate to be going back."

"Go back so that you may keep in the battle for souls," Franson commanded. The young man straightened up and walked toward his litter. A wave of the hand, and Franson was left alone.

Alone, and yet not alone. On the long marches he communed with his heavenly Father. He continued to make friends with the men in the caravan, using gestures and facial expressions to convey his ideas. On the stops along the way he kept up the same pantomime.

At one inn where he was offered food, he was afraid it might be pork which he did not like. He said, "Oink oink!" and wrinkled up his nose, trying to act out the part of a pig, and pushed his hands away as in refusal. The innkeeper caught on immediately and grinned broadly. "Baa, baa," he said, and shortly Franson was feasting on mutton stew.

The privations of the road were nothing to him. He had always lived a simple life. Moreover, he rejoiced to face some of the same hardships that were common to those whom he had sent to the mission field. It was not discomfort and danger that appealed to him, but the sense of working together with his hallelujah soldiers to win men to Jesus Christ.

Chapter 26

FORWARD UNTIL UPWARD

ANNIE OLSON beat time to the music with wide arcs and sweeping flourishes. She led the singing at the Scandinavian Alliance Mission conference with all the skill of an experienced Salvation Army officer. Her days with the Minneapolis corps were not forgotten.

She began to clap her hands to accompany the singing. "Come on, everybody," she cried, "clap your hands along with me. If I see anyone not clapping, we will stop."

Facing that ultimatum, everyone joined her, including Franson, and the building reverberated with the marching songs of faith. This was still a young group of missionaries, and they sang with spirit.

Gathered in from the sixteen stations in Shensi, three others in Shensi and four places in Kansu, the missionaries looked forward to the help and advice their mission leader could give them.

When Franson rose to speak, he looked slowly from left to right. Then he said, "My old comrades, how good it is to be with you once again. I know that some are missing, but they are praising God before His throne on high and praising our dear Saviour. It was placed on my heart and mind today to speak about the Lord Jesus Christ, for He is the One who leads us on.

"We sinners, we rebels who have no way to save ourselves, it is us He loved. He took our burden for the purpose that we should witness for Him. The burden is on
us to make Him known.

"Christ can make a gift of us and of our lives to the
lost. Lord grant vision that our hearts be opened and
Christ afresh be revealed, more precious than ever before."

Throughout the conference he continued to inspire the
missionaries and counsel them. Two matters were uppermost in his mind.

"I urge you to do the thing which I have done so often
in the home countries," he said. "That is, to hold Bible
courses among the Christians to deepen their spiritual
life and to train lay evangelists. You will never reach the
masses around you unless you have a witnessing church.
It is not enough to get up in meetings and tell the Christians to witness. Only concentrated courses of Bible study,
fellowship in prayer for the unsaved, and participation
with you in street preaching and home visitation will prepare them for action.

"The other great need is for a seminary to train pastors
and teachers for the churches. The leaders you have in
the churches need a better knowledge of the Word of God.
Now how do you think you could go about this?"

The missionaries agreed enthusiastically to open a seminary in Sian, and they began to schedule short-term Bible
schools for their districts.

"I am delighted with the literature you have printed on
the Sian press," Franson said, "and I hope this is but a
beginning of a flood of Christian books and tracts."

He was concerned too about the children of missionaries. "The school at Chefoo is a wonderful place," he declared. "God blessed us with revival among the boys and

girls when I was there. It is such a long way to the sea-coast, however, I have been thinking that perhaps you should have a school for your children right here."

The parents were overjoyed with this prospect, and the mission school opened that very fall in Pinglian. Franson always had time for the children, even in the midst of business matters. At one time in the home of John and Kristina Nelson he interrupted mission questions to gather their children around him. "What are your names?" he asked.

When he learned that they were called Ruth, Arthur, and Esther, he placed his hands on their heads and prayed that they would grow up to be missionaries like their parents. "O Christ, our blessed Redeemer, bless these dear children," he prayed. "Have Thy good hand upon them. Perform Thy own loving will and purpose. Oh, that they may follow Thee, to serve Thee; most of all, for Thy pleasing, O Lord, to be blessed by Thee and be a blessing to others. And so, Lord, thou shalt perform more than we ask or think. In Jesus' blessed name. Amen."

These three children grew up to be missionaries in China, both in Shensi and later in Taiwan (Formosa), the beginning of a second generation on the mission fields of The Evangelical Alliance Mission.

Following the mission conference, Franson withdrew with William Englund and some other missionaries for a time of rest in the hills. There, as was his custom, he spent hours in prayer out in solitary spots. This greatly impressed the priests at the local temple, and they remembered this man of prayer for years afterward.

Then, refreshed and ready for a ministry on the Sian plain, Franson began meetings in the Chinese churches. In one of his first messages he spoke to a large audience about the second coming of Christ. Many were moved to repentance by what he said, but one non-Christian, who listened intently, gloated to a neighbor, "That is fine that all the Christians at the mission station will disappear, for then I can take their horse!"

Franson laughed when this was reported to him, but he used the incident in his next letter to praying friends in the homelands. "This Chinese took the matter seriously even though his only thought was selfish gain," he wrote. "Who will get what you leave when Jesus comes? Do you not think you could send part of it beforehand to heaven by way of our treasurers of the Mission, and do it at once?"

Although Franson wanted Christians in the homelands to support missionary work, he had an eye to local support and the development of indigenous churches. When he met Annie Olson again at her station, Sang-kia-chuang, he found her somewhat discouraged by the lawless condition of the countryside and the slow progress among the believers. At the time she had services in rented premises, but Franson prophesied that God had something better for her. Taking her out for a walk one day, he pointed to a plot of land and said, "The station will stand there one day."

"I don't have the funds to build," she replied. "Where will the money come from?"

"The Chinese will provide it," he said.

God used unusual means to bring this to pass. A man lost a mule and asked Miss Olson to intercede with the magistrate to help locate it. Instead she said she would pray, and, after prayer, he recovered his mule. The whole town was excited by this story, and as a result of it a wealthy businessman was converted. He owned the very lot which Franson had pointed out, and one day he came to Miss Olson to announce that he was donating this land for the church and mission. He also moved a large ancestral hall and reconstructed it on this property for a church building.

Franson had proceeded around the field. After a meeting which he held in Wukung, many women stayed behind as inquirers. While they talked with the missionary, Christina Anderson, Franson walked up and down in the background, praying and exclaiming, "Dear God! Praise God!"

After the women had gone home, he met Miss Anderson with the words, "Have they gone? See, sister, what God can do! Tell me, are you willing to offer yourself wholly for the women of China?"

Tears filled her eyes. "Dear brother Franson, what more can I do? I have left home and friends and all."

"It was not that I asked about, my sister, but whether you are willing to offer all for the women of China."

"Yes, I am willing to do what is God's will," she answered.

When he was leaving the station his last words were "Remember what you promised, sister; God will show you the way."

From this encounter sprang large, new steps of faith by Miss Anderson. She saw the great need for schools for young women and developed, under God, the outstanding Bible training institutions for women in Hingping.

Franson liked the Chinese prayer meetings where all prayed in unison. "Ah," he remarked, "my English or Swedish can mingle freely with the Chinese as we all pray together, and our praise then ascends on high."

It was in these times of close fellowship with the Chinese brethren that he became even more burdened for their Bible training. Thus he rejoiced when a letter came from Katherine Juell of Norway with news of a large gift from her for the seminary property. "Now that I have heard of this answer to prayer, I can go on my way happily," he said.

Wilhelm Hagquist, who was with him, inquired, "What are your plans?"

"I still have some meetings in mission stations down-country. Then I continue around the world visiting our fields. I have already been on the way two years, and I don't know how much longer it will take."

"Please, be careful," Hagquist warned. "Fredrickson has died in India. There are fevers in Africa. How do you know that you will live to complete this tour?"

Franson was positive. "I have had a definite assurance from God that I will be permitted to make this tour, but after that I have no plan."

Later as he traveled down the Yangtze through the famous Szechuan gorges, he was without foreign companions. Nevertheless, he exulted in the experience. Writing to thank Miss Juell for her gift toward the seminary, he told her about his trip:

> The foaming waters over which the little boat literally flew like a bird, the towering walls of the mountains, the bracing winds, the echo of the voices of the boatmen when they called to each other, the solitude, especially during the nights, in my little hired boat—all this combined to touch the vibrating strings of the heart, so that I could only exclaim, sometimes in a loud voice, 'God is in His temple, and I am with Him there.'

Chapter 27

REVIVAL IN ARMENIA

S EVERAL MONTHS LATER (in the year 1904) Franson visited the India-Tibetan frontier field where the work had been proceeding slowly. This time his enthusiasm turned to the teeming plains of India where vast populations awaited the gospel. After a three-week visit among the Bhils in West Khandesh, he wrote back to the Dahlgrens at Ghoom, urging them to move from the Tibetan work to this needy field. They made the transfer, and this was the beginning of TEAM's large field northeast of Bombay.

By the time he was ready to leave India, Franson had visited every station and all the workers of the Scandinavian Alliance Mission, baptizing altogether one hundred and sixty converts. At this point, instead of going directly to the South Africa field, he visited the Bible lands of Mesopotamia, stopping at Baghdad and the ruins of Babylon. Then, on invitation of the American Board, Franson moved into Turkey for meetings among the Armenians. At Mardin more than a hundred were converted as he preached, and this was the beginning of one of the greatest revivals in which he was used.

Dr. Atkinson, the American Board missionary who welcomed Franson, looked him over and then commented, "Excuse my mentioning the similarity, but you look almost exactly like Charles Dickens, Mr. Franson!"

Franson smiled broadly.

"Yes, that's it. You both look remarkably cheery," Atkinson continued. "I mean it as a compliment. Well, we consider ourselves fortunate to have you. It is not very customary for the head of a missionary organization to be doing general evangelistic work."

"I can explain that," Franson answered. "I found that I could best interest the churches at home by holding revival meetings first and then presenting the cause of missions. And I have found that the best way to help mission churches is to hold revival meetings in them wherever I go."

Their talk turned to revival, and he added, "Finney always recognized that God uses every faithful Christian in revival as well as leaders. He told of a stammering blacksmith who closed his shop one Friday and prayed for revival. The next Sunday a revival broke out, and the young people who came under conviction testified that they had all begun to feel uncomfortable about their sins on the previous Friday. That was when the blacksmith was praying. I am sure that you have some praying people at Mardin, and that is the reason we saw such remarkable results there."

Franson found another prepared place when he reached the city of Marash. The believers had been praying for weeks that God would bless them with revival. With his very first message the Holy Spirit began to work mightily. A heaven-sent revival broke out. Soon even drunkards, gamblers, and criminals were irresistibly drawn into the services. They came, they felt the convicting and regenerating power of the Holy Spirit, they were conquered and converted. The conversion and transformation of such notorious sinners left a tremendous impression on the city.

The revival kept on for six weeks. One young church member named Elmajian watched the proceedings with mounting disapproval. He had a high opinion of his own righteousness, and he decided not to attend the meetings anymore. He couldn't keep away, however. At last one night he too walked forward and, kneeling down as a sinner, found glorious salvation.

Franson looked deep in his eyes and said, "God wants you to go out now and witness for Jesus Christ."

The next day Elmajian witnessed to a group of his classmates, and six of them immediately accepted Christ. These fellows followed the Lord faithfully, dying some years later as martyrs in the Turkish massacres.

The revival in Armenia under Franson was so tremendous that even when he had no interpreter, waves of conviction came over the people. He would gather crowds in the streets. As they gazed in amazement at this strange foreigner, he would point heavenward. The look on his face would bring them to their knees, and then the local Christians dealt with them.

Franson spent six months in this ministry before finally taking passage in Beirut, Syria, for South Africa. He landed at Durban and went inland to the SAM field. Malla Moe was on furlough, but eleven other missionaries were there to greet him. After the setbacks of the early years, the Mission had developed four main stations and forty outstations, fifty self-supporting evangelists, and twenty-eight evangelists who were partially supported.

Franson announced a Bible course for African believers, and group after group came from different localities, singing hymns as they marched in to the central station. During the Bible course he had revival meetings in the evenings. Many of the unsaved thronged in and were converted. At the end of the Bible course he baptized fifty-six of the best students whom the missionaries considered sufficiently instructed to receive baptism.

Moving on to other parts of South Africa, Franson had a wide ministry among the different races there. He spent a week in the home of Andrew Murray, the leading evangelical Bible teacher and writer and an ardent supporter of missionary work. Murray was seventy-nine years old, but still preaching occasionally. He gladly introduced Franson to the Dutch Reformed chuches, not only in South Africa but also in South America, where scattered groups of Boers had resettled. Dr. Murray's daughter helped with this correspondence, and with other letters which Franson needed to send off.

By August, 1907, the American evangelist was ready to leave South Africa. He wrote the Chicago headquarters of the Mission, "Now farewell to South Africa and welcome to South America! As time goes on I will sometime and somewhere turn up in North America, probably before the end of this year—that is, if the heavenly Lightning Express does not come before that time to fetch us all up yonder."

His campaigns in South America began in Buenos Aires, Argentina, and covered most of the countries on that continent. Word of the spiritual effectiveness of his ministry sped ahead of him and served as his credentials, opening churches of many different denominations to him. One Sunday morning in Rio Grande do Sul, Brazil, he preached in a black robe at a German Lutheran service and then in white vestments at an Anglican service in the evening.

When someone asked how someone with his free church background could do this, he answered, "The Father is to be worshiped in spirit and in truth. Now, as I always have, I try to take with me the Spirit of God and the truth of the Word. Then it matters very little whether I am dressed in ministerial regalia or appear in my shirt sleeves."

Through Uruguay, Chile, and Peru he moved, heading toward his own Mission's new field in Venezuela. He had heard with delight of the arrival of the T. J. Bachs and the John Christiansens in Maracaibo, but he had been in South America almost a year before he reached them. In March, 1908, they met, and Franson grasped both Bach and Christiansen warmly by the hand. "You are the first missionaries," he said, "but many more will come."

He was all encouragement for the printing press and the little magazine *La Estrella de la Mañana*. He rejoiced to dedicate the mission launch which would take the missionaries to many villages around Lake Maracaibo.

The mission hall at that time was just a wide porch in the missionaries' home—a small platform and pulpit, the folding organ, and some potted plants at the front, and then rows of straight-backed chairs.

Every night the room was crowded as Franson preached and the young men interpreted. Once a gang of rowdies sat at the back, laughed and joked, and tried to break up the meeting. After the meeting Christiansen rushed up to tell Bach and Franson that a good many of the cane seats had been slashed and were ruined. The three of them went back to inspect the damage.

Bach's neck reddened with embarrassment and anger. "What shall we do? Call the police?" he asked.

Franson was unperturbed. He held up his hand. "No, no, don't do that," he cautioned. "I know a better way. Here, let's count how many holes there are."

Wondering what he meant, Bach and Christiansen did so and found that there were seventy holes.

"All right," Franson said, "let's kneel down and pray that God will give us one soul for every hole, seventy in all."

The young missionaries' indignation simmered down, and before long they were praying as fervently as their mission leader for the souls of those young men. In the days that followed they welcomed each new conversion with a cheer, "Praise God, that's one of the seventy!"

The day came when Franson told his co-workers, "Soon I must pack my little bag, and say good-bye to you."

"Where will you go from here?" they asked.

"I don't know exactly where—Curaçao, Jamaica, Cuba, perhaps Mexico, before I get home. The Lord knows. My motto these days is 'Forward until upward.' "

He lifted his finger in the air. "Remember it, my dear brothers," he said. "I pass it on to you. 'Forward until upward.' "

Chapter 28

ON THE ALTAR

F RANSON BRISKLY handed his American citizenship papers
to the official at the Brownsville, Texas, border. The in-
spector gave the well-worn sheets a cursory examination
and handed them back. Franson folded them with care
and tucked them in an inside pocket. Arriving thus from
Mexico, he was again in his homeland after an absence of
nearly six years.

Though unheralded and without anyone to greet him at
this point, he expected to meet friends in Austin, the state
capital. It was Friday, June 5, 1908, and he could reach
their home for the weekend.

On the way across Texas he watched the unfolding
landscape with concentration and delight. He noted fami-
liar-looking main streets, laundry flapping on backyard
lines, and country church steeples. This was home, and he
reveled in it. Then he saw some cotton fields with Negro
hands hoeing between the rows, and this was new to him.
He had never been in this section of the country before.

Franson was happy at the sight of the Reverend Alfred
Stone and his wife when the train pulled in to the Austin
station. They too recognized him with ease. The pastor
came toward him with open arms and the words "Welcome, and God's peace!"

177

Franson put his arm around him and smiled at the others who had come, saying, "So now I am among my dear Swedish friends again, praise God!"

"Yes, and there will be more wanting to hear about your missionary travels," brother Stone told him. "We hope you will preach in the Swedish church in Kilroy this Sunday."

"It will be a blessed joy, dear brother," Franson replied.

"I think I have something right here that will bring joy to your heart," Stone added, reaching into his coat pocket and pulling out a packet of letters. "These have been accumulating for you for some days."

Franson untied the string and looked them over one by one. "Risberg—Dyrness—Youngberg—Bach," he said to himself. Then noticing the others waiting around him, he said, "Wonderful! Wonderful! Well, let's be going."

On Sunday Franson preached with great power about the masses of people without Christ whom he had seen in foreign lands. "This whole world is the vineyard entrusted to our care. The Master is coming back to see what we have been doing," he declared. "Would you be ready if He came today? Or would you be among those servants who will be ashamed because of their carelessness, their sloth, and their indifference?"

Tears began to flow in the congregation as he pressed the danger to lost souls when Christians fail to witness to them. This master soul-winner had one aim as he preached to these Christian people, and that was to create a conscience and a passion for the souls of men among them.

The next day he was out on the streets, distributing tracts and speaking at length to passersby, both white and colored. At dinner that day he remarked to his friends, "I note a difference here in the attitude between the races from that which I have seen so recently down in the West Indies."

"In what way do you mean, Pastor Franson?" they asked.

"Well, in the Caribbean Islands and on the South American mainland the colored mingle freely with white people. You don't see separate drinking fountains and other facilities as you do here."

"We have found it the custom in these parts," someone said, "and we don't think much about it."

"I expect the Negroes think quite a bit about it," Franson persisted, "and I have a good idea what the Lord thinks about it. Now when I was in Jamaica I had dinner with a Negro pastor in his home in Kingston. He was a Presbyterian and a lovely Christian. No one thought it strange that we should eat together."

"Really?" his hostess remarked. "I can't imagine such a thing."

"Yes, really," Franson said. "And when I was on the Dutch island of Curaçao, I was introduced to a Negro lady to whom the people there gave great deference. She was a British citizen and had received the Order of the British Empire."

There was a lull in the conversation until Franson changed the subject, saying, "The dear brethren in the home office of the Scandinavian Alliance Mission urge me to come to Chicago at once."

"Will you go, Brother Franson?" he was asked.

"I think not. Not yet," he said. "I would like to see them again, even as I would like to see my dear family in Nebraska. It may seem strange to delay going, but the Lord seems to be telling me to spend some weeks of rest up in Colorado before I go any farther."

"Have you any plans for this fall and winter?" Mr. Stone asked.

"Yes, I have a plan," he replied. "God willing, I am going to travel all over our beloved United States. I want to use the watchword 'Children and Young People for Christ,' and especially hold youth meetings."

The next week he bade his friends farewell and headed north. Reaching Denver, Colorado, he boarded another train for Boulder. There among the Rockies he loved, he began to rest. On June 17 he passed his fifty-sixth birthday without mentioning it to anyone. "I'm getting older," he thought to himself, "and just that much closer to heaven."

He had been more tired than he realized, but he wanted renewed strength. Turning to Psalm 121 day by day, he read, "I will lift up mine eyes unto the hills. From whence cometh my help? My help cometh from the Lord, which made heaven and earth. . .The Lord shall preserve thy going out and thy coming in from this time forth, and even for evermore."

He began to feel a refreshing touch on his weary body. When he received a letter the next week inviting him to take a summer pastorate at Idaho Springs, he rejoiced at the possibility of more time in the mountains. Rev. Oscar Bolander, a young Covenant minister whom he had met some years previously in Rockford, Illinois, was writing. He was just leaving the Covenant Church in Idaho Springs to take up a new charge at Boulder. Learning that Franson was there, he would be coming over on July 1 to see if he would supply the church Bolander was leaving, at least for a few weeks. The deacons had asked him to approach Franson.

Idaho Springs—what memories this brought back. Franson had been there ten years before. He thought of the revival meetings, packed out with miners . . . the young man Carlson whom he had led to Christ after a wild chase . . . that bubbling spring where he had given a young lady a tin mug of water and told her about the springs of life in Christ. He would like to go back if God would permit it.

When the young pastor came to Boulder he had meetings scheduled which he shared with Franson. In between times they talked about the Idaho Springs church. "The numbers are less than they used to be," Bolander said. "Some of the mines have shut down and then church members moved away. If you can come and help for a while, it will mean so much to those that are left. They're grand people. I'm sorry to be leaving them."

"There were only a handful of members when I was there for meetings," Franson said, "but God gave us some good times. He filled the empty pews with unsaved people, and many of them found Christ."

"You'll come then, won't you?" Bolander pled.

"You don't need to convince me," Franson answered. "I've been praying about it, and then the Lord was good enough to send a letter from the Mission telling me to take all the time up here I needed. I'll go back with you."

He agreed to serve as supply preacher for one month. The deacons already had a place for him in the home of a widow, Mrs. Mathilda Swanson. She showed him with pride into the best room in her small frame cottage. "The windows have a good view of the valley and the hills," she explained.

Franson set down his small bag and thanked her for her hospitality. Then he set out with Bolander to visit in some of the homes of church members. As the two men climbed up the steep streets, Franson commented on changes in the town. "These sidewalks are a great improvement," he said. Then just as suddenly he asked, "Bolander, have you ever thought of going to the heathen?"

The young man was taken back and wondered for a moment if perhaps he was a slacker. Then he managed to say, "So far as I know, Brother Franson, the Lord has not given a call, and without a call I would not venture to think about it."

Franson cocked his head slightly to one side, then nodded and said, "Very well. Ve-ry well! I suppose some have to remain to attend to the work at home."

Later as Bolander was leaving for his new charge, Franson took him aside and said, "You are just twenty-seven years old, and you should have great opportunities with the young people at Boulder. We need to be reaching youth for Christ. Dear brother, don't neglect them."

After Bolander's departure Franson walked home by way of the Bostrom place. Mr. Bostrom was the most active deacon and also superintendent of the Sunday school. "Tomorrow will be our first Sunday working together," Franson said to him. "Let us pray for the children who will come."

Bostrom agreed readily to this suggestion. "I think that we will have quite a few new ones," he said. "The word is getting around that a missionary has come, and the children love to hear a missionary."

During the weeks that followed, Franson carried on the work of the church, so much so that Mrs. Swanson chided him, "Pastor, you are doing too much. You came here for a rest."

"Now don't you worry," he said. "I've got to work off some of the good food you give me."

One Saturday evening he shared a service in the church with another visiting missionary whom he had met before in India. A large crowd had come, but Bostrom was working on night shift and could not attend. In the course of the meeting Franson led in prayer. He asked with great earnestness that God endue Bostrom with gifts for Christian service. "Lord, dear Lord," he prayed, "Thou knowest that I will soon be leaving this church. Do lay Thy hand on Brother Bostrom and enable him to minister Thy Word to Thy people."

When Mrs. Bostrom told her husband what Franson had prayed, he was deeply impressed. He knelt right down and asked God to fulfill Franson's prayer in his life.

If he had heard, Franson would have rejoiced. He had sensed aright that this Christian brother was open to the Lord's leading. Already God was beginning a fresh work in Idaho Springs. He was answering prayer.

Franson's prayers ranged over the world as usual, but in particular he prayed for the rising generation in America. He spent hours in his room, planning and meditating on the work he hoped to do with them. Then he wrote a letter for publication in the church papers announcing his hopes for youth meetings in many parts of the country.

At other times he took long walks up toward the nearby peaks, carrying his Bible and bulky prayer list with him. Mrs. Swanson asked no questions, but she noticed the peace and joy on his face when he returned.

At supper one night he volunteered the information that he had built an altar on the mountaintop. "I gathered some rocks together in a cairn," he said, "and placed a flat slab on top."

Mrs. Swanson put her fork down on her plate and looked at him in amazement. "What did you do that for?" she asked.

"Just for the thrill of doing something like the old men of God in the Bible did. That's what they did to show their love for God." Franson looked steadily at her. Could he trust her with a confidence? He went on. "When I am up there on the mountain with God, He tells me to look northward, southward, eastward, and westward at all the land which He is giving me to witness in. Look, let me show you in the Bible."

Franson quickly turned to Genesis 13. Holding the Bible to the light, he read, "Arise, walk through the land in the length and in the breadth of it; for I will give it unto thee. Then Abram removed his tent, and came and dwelt . . . in Hebron, and built there an altar unto the Lord."

One day when he had walked in another direction, he came back and reported with a smile, "I built another altar today."

"You shouldn't be lifting heavy rocks, Pastor Franson," Mrs. Swanson remonstrated. "You were panting when you came up the steps and into the house."

"Thank you for your concern for me, Sister Swanson," he replied, "but it's this way. I think of all the mounds of prayer stones I have seen built by the heathen for their gods, and it makes me want to raise something dedicated to the true God of heaven and all the earth."

Franson's time in Idaho Springs was drawing to a close. On Friday evening, July 31, he met with the deacons in the church and encouraged them to trust the Lord for the future. He was in high spirits and led them in fervent prayer. At the end he lingered for a while talking with Mr. Bostrom in front of the church while the others disappeared into the shadows. "My brother," Franson said, "I'm happy because I know what God can do in and through you. Just remember that constant, close communion is the key to blessing from the Lord."

Climbing up the mountainside on Saturday, he thought to himself, *This will be my last visit up here. My month that God has given me is almost up.* He noted the wild flowers, yellow, white, and pink. *They have nothing quite as wonderful as you in Chicago,* he mused.

He approached the altar he had built. Here he could look in all directions, seeing range upon range of distant peaks, some of them crowned with snow. The cool winds whipped his beard and ruffled the flaps of his coat.

He put his Bible and prayer list down in a niche between the rocks, out of the wind. Then he knelt down to pray once more. He had prayed here for others. He had prayed for himself. Sometimes he had sung the old hymns. This day he was silent.

What do you have to say to me, dear loving Lord? was the unspoken query of his heart. He was ready for any fresh onslaught now against the enemy of souls. What new venture, what new attack was his commission? The answer crept in. He should be ready for anything, even what he might not want. Would he once again lay his all on the altar of God's will?

"Why, yes, Lord," he said. "Whatever Thy will is, wherever the road may lead, just so long as I can be with Thee."

That evening he retired early. The next morning when he did not appear for breakfast and no sound of stirring came from his room, Mrs. Swanson finally knocked on his door.

"Come in," she heard.

She opened the door slowly. Franson was lying in bed

with his hands folded together on his chest. He was look-ing straight up and did not turn to look at her.

"Are you all right, Pastor Franson?" she said anxiously.

"Yes, I'm all right" and he paused. "I've had this pain before, and it has passed."

"Shall I call the doctor?"

"No, there is nothing he can do for me now. God is my doctor."

Mrs. Swanson quietly closed the door, hastened outside, and, picking up her skirts, hurried to the nearest tele-phone. She called Dr. Morehouse, who said he would be over immediately. The word spread along the party line, and, though the doctor's buggy reached Mrs. Swanson's home first, Brother Bostrom, John Lofvenberg, Alfred Hector, and Alfred Freeman were not far behind.

Franson's eyes were closed, and Dr. Morehouse had already checked his heart with his stethoscope. He shook his head slowly. "There is nothing I can do," he said. "He has already gone beyond."

The men stood silently around the bed, not in grief so much as awe. A great peace filled the room. Then Bostrom picked up Franson's Bible and fingered it lovingly.

He turned the pages to I Corinthians 15 and said, "I think it would be fitting to read a passage from God's Word which our brother must have read many times:

> Behold, I shew you a mystery; we shall not all sleep, but we shall all be changed, in a moment, in the twinkling of an eye, at the last trump; for the trumpet shall sound, and the dead shall be raised incorruptible, and we shall be changed. . . . O death, where is thy sting? O grave, where is thy victory? The sting of death is sin; and the strength of sin is the law. But thanks be to God, which giveth us the victory through

our Lord Jesus Christ. Therefore, my beloved brethren, be ye stedfast, unmovable, always abounding in
the work of the Lord, forasmuch as ye know that your
labor is not in vain in the Lord.

They knelt in prayer. The sunshine poured in on the
bowed heads, the frayed carpet, and the silent figure on
the bed. Bostrom had a catch in his voice as he prayed,
"Dear God, Thou dost know what a blessing Thy servant
has been to us, showing us a love for Thee and for us and
for the poor, lost sinners, a love greater than we have ever
known. Help us as Thou hast helped him, so that we
can preach Thy gospel too, till Jesus comes. Even so come,
Lord Jesus."

And the others said, "Amen."

Chapter 29

HE STILL SPEAKS

WHAT HAS HAPPENED to Franson's vision of a witness throughout the United States? What about the widespread missionary activities in all parts of the world? Would they suffer without his leadership?

It has been said that God buries His saints, but His work goes on. Fredrik Franson's body lies in an honored spot beside those of other missionary pioneers in the Mount Olivet Cemetery, Chicago. It awaits that glad resurrection day when Jesus comes. Meanwhile, for Franson himself it has been "absent from the body, present with the Lord." What a home-coming that must have been! It is not for us to know now the details of his reception in heaven, but we can know about the work he left behind.

He was a worker together with God, and thus his influence has continued and is increasing. His words and work are not forgotten. He had a ministry of prayer, and some of his prayers are still being answered. He had a ministry in the hearts of men, and they are still responding to his rallying cry. He had a spirit of love which placed its stamp on those who knew him. Perhaps the best known of these was Dr. T. J. Bach, who also was the general director of The Evangelical Alliance Mission for many years. To know these men is to know in some measure what Franson was like.

The Mission he left behind has spread beyond Scandinavian circles in the United States until now it is well known everywhere. Its 850 missionaries overseas are a potent force for world evangelization that would delight Franson's heart. This growth is not only a living monument to his vision and skill as a founder of missions, it is a testimony to the principles by which he lived.

Franson never wanted praise for himself. Whatever he had learned, he had learned from Christ. It is only so far as we can see Jesus Christ operative in his life that it is instructive for us. He wielded a wide influence in his lifetime. Others wanted to enter into the same life he had. They wanted to share his joys. They saw in Franson a man of God who could teach them many lessons.

We too can look for the key to his life of power. This does not mean that we will duplicate everything Franson did. God gives His servants different tasks. We may be led in different ways, but there is only one basic relationship possible between ourselves and our Lord.

Franson knew this. It was the relationship of a willing and obedient servant. The key to his life was his complete surrender to the will of God. He was determined to do God's work in God's way and with God's supply of grace. He knew how to lay his innermost struggles down at the foot of the cross, and go on his way rejoicing.

What a man! He had the remarkable intensity of the single-minded. "This one thing I do" was his motto, and what he did was not out of grinding duty or for driving ambition. It was for the joy of the Lord. He was thrilled with the tasks God gave him to do. There was no holding back from God, but a gay thrusting forward into each fresh adventure.

Moreover, he was paying the price of a walk with God. Thus at the heart of his exuberance lay a sober estimate of sin and Satan. He faced undaunted the realities of the world and also of the unseen world. They drove him to an ever firmer reliance on Christ.

Franson encourages us even where we cannot possibly copy him. He was a farmer's son who moved at ease with royalty. He became a learned man who still talked freely with unlettered peasants. Though a poor man, he channeled large amounts of money to good and useful ends. He was much alone and much with people. He commanded respect without losing the common touch. He was a preoccupied man at times, and yet he was ever alert for spiritual opportunities.

What is the sum of such a life? What can we appropriate for ourselves from Franson's example? First of all, it breathes the fragrance of Franson's Lord. The Lord Jesus gives so much if we will but have it. We too can have a life of prayer, a heart of love, a passion for souls, a delight in God's Word, a faith that attempts the impossible, a fearlessness which escapes convention, and the great goal of Christ's soon return.

This devotion to Christ also shines as a light in the world's darkness. We need more lights burning for Jesus. And what is the assurance we have that God will do this? The missionary evangelists trained by Franson would probably have expressed it with the strum of a guitar and the words of a Swedish hymn:

> Though He giveth or He taketh,
> God His children ne'er forsaketh,
> His the loving purpose solely
> To preserve them pure and holy.